For Anya and John

KV-681-707

FROM EGG
TO ADOLESCENT

Xenopus – a model for development

LOUIE HAMILTON, M.A., Ph.D.,
Department of Biology as applied to Medicine,
The Middlesex Hospital Medical School

THE ENGLISH UNIVERSITIES PRESS LTD

591.33
HAM

added £
597.6

51
√√

CJ101169

CHRIST'S COLLEGE
LIBRARY LINE STACK

Access on No. 56565

Class No. 591.33
HAM

Catal.

7.9.76   CE

ISBN 0 340 15497 7

First printed 1976

Copyright © 1976 Louie Hamilton
All rights reserved. No part of this publication may be reproduced
or transmitted in any form or by any means, electronic or mechanical,
including photocopy, recording or any information storage or retrieval
system, without permission in writing from the publisher.

The English Universities Press Ltd
St Paul's House, Warwick Lane, London EC4P 4AH

Printed in Great Britain by
Elliott Bros. & Yeoman Ltd., Liverpool L24 9JL

Foreword

Among laboratory workers I think that only an embryologist would ever describe it as a principal recommendation of the organism he studies that it is as an outstandingly beautiful object. It is most revealing and ingratiating that embryologists should do so, but good embryologists do indeed look upon the developmental process with something like awe. I can still remember my wonder and amazement the first time I saw a 3-day chick embryo in its shell. In retrospect it makes me wonder, as embryologists do constantly wonder, how biologists can ever bring themselves to study any lesser phenomenon than the unfolding of development from egg to adult.

Embryology has passed through quite a number of conceptual revolutions in its day. In the heyday of comparative anatomy it was quite widely believed that embryology would yield up all its secrets to conventional methods of histology and microscopy, i.e. the cutting and staining of sections and their investigation under the ordinary light microscope. For this reason they missed altogether the remarkable and distinctive characteristic of early development, that it is above all else a *kinetic* process distinguished by the relative movements of columns and sheets of cells by the activities that Oliver Wendell Holmes likened to those of a glass blower who, starting with a tube, can produce creases and grooves and ridges and inpushings and outpushings somewhat analogous to those that occur in early development. To these fundamental processes Dr Hamilton naturally pays special attention. It was Wilhelm Vogt who discovered these cellular movements by the device—simple in principle, but not all that easy to execute—of colouring groups of cells with harmless dyes which made it possible to trace their movements in the embryo: it was in principle impossible for conventional microtomy and microscopy to reveal these fundamental processes. It is just because so much of the tactics of early development is a matter of relative cell movement that the embryo is of necessity laid out in the form of flattened envelopes of cells—the germ layers to which classical embryologists paid such very serious attention;

not realising, of course, that their significance is essentially a tactical one. A second great conceptual revolution in embryology came about when embryologists began to realise the highly important part played by the blastopore (Chap. 3) in the processes of gastrulation and neurulation which together form the great metamorphosis common to all chordate animals, as a consequence of which the embryo becomes a sort of prototypical chordate, with head and tail and median dorsal hollow nerve tube with a skeletal rod, the notochord, lying just below it. Transplantation experiments by Spemann and his colleagues showed that the tubular central nervous system arose as a result of some influence emanating from the roof of the gut formed by the process of invagination. The formation of the three primary sub-divisions of the brain, of the segmental muscle blocks and the embryonic kidneys all follow the glass blowing type of morphogenesis.

The third revolution that affected embryology was that which at the same time affected every other branch of biology: it was a consequence of the discovery that information flow in biosynthesis could proceed only in the direction from nucleic acid to protein or other macromolecule. This discovery places the burden of specifying development wholly upon the nucleus of the cell. The classical experiments of Hans Driesch taken in conjunction with experiments of equal stature carried out by Gurdon more recently have made it clear that the divisions of the zygote nucleus are genetically equal, and that each cell in the developing embryo has the same genetic makeup and therefore the same genetic information. Because of this discovery cellular differentiation is now generally interpreted as the process by which some one innate capability of the cell is realised while others lie dormant or are perhaps suppressed.

The attraction of Dr Hamilton's book is that it is not a specialised embryological text in any of the conventional senses, i.e. it is not a work of 'experimental embryology' devoted essentially to an attempt to make sense out of a huge variety of experiments in transplantation and various forms of experimental interference with development; nor is it a 'molecular embryology' in which a brave attempt is made to interpret cellular movements and cellular affinities in terms of the molecular makeup of cellular membranes. Least of all is it a traditional embryological text illustrated by photographs of innumerable transverse sections of embryos at various stages. Rather it is a judicious combination of all of these, the work as a whole making an admirable text book of general embryology which is all the more realistic for being grounded upon the study of a single organism: *Xenopus laevis* has been a most admirable colleague.

P. B. Medawar

Contents

Acknowledgements

I should like to thank all the unnamed people who have helped me by commenting on this book in preparation. Many are my potential readers, i.e. trainee school teachers, sixth formers and university students. I should, however like to thank the following by name for their help with the illustrations: Mrs Julia Hunt, Dr J G Bluemink, Dr R Coleman, Mr P Drury, Dr H Fox, Academic Press and the Company of Biologists.

I should also like to express my gratitude to Mr F T C Harris and Mrs C Morgan for helping in different ways with the preparation of the manuscript.

Louie Hamilton

Introduction

PERHAPS the greatest attraction of *Xenopus* is the beauty of its embryo. When to this is added the convenience of inducing *Xenopus* to mate at any time of the year and of studying its minutest developmental stages with a low power microscope, it can be seen why it provides such a popular vehicle for both teaching and research.

As with other amphibians the egg and embryo are an ideal size for study, being neither too small nor too large. However, this is only an overall assessment because in some respects the egg is too big and yolky thus making it impossible to observe the early cell movements of the living embryo with the aid of the phase contrast microscope. In other ways the egg is too small and develops too fast to make the collection of particular cell samples for biochemical analysis easy. The overriding advantages are that fertilisation is external and the embryos and larvae may thereafter be grown at room temperature. It is possible to remove the membranes from an early embryo in order to operate on it and then to keep it to the hatching stage under relatively simple conditions.

50 mm

Fig. 1
Adult male (right) and female (left) *Xenopus*. Dorsal view. (By courtesy of Dr R. Coleman)

In this book the development of the South African Clawed Toad (*Xenopus laevis*) (Fig. 1) is the basis of the narrative. Recent descriptions of particular facets of development include the results of electronmicroscopic and biochemical investigations. These are described together with those experiments that throw light on the complex processes of development. In writing the descriptive material I have drawn extensively on the detailed morphological account of development to be found in 'The Normal Table of *Xenopus laevis* (Daudin)' edited by Nieuwkoop and Faber and first published in 1956. I always refer to their standardised, and now internationally recognised, stages of development (Fig. 2).

(a) 0–2¾h

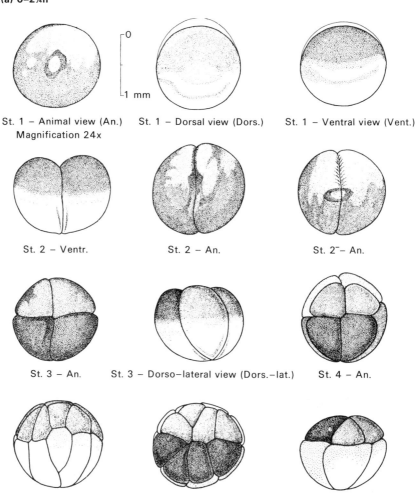

St. 1 – Animal view (An.)   St. 1 – Dorsal view (Dors.)   St. 1 – Ventral view (Vent.)
Magnification 24x

St. 2 – Ventr.   St. 2 – An.   St. 2⁻– An.

St. 3 – An.   St. 3 – Dorso–lateral view (Dors.–lat.)   St. 4 – An.

St. 5 – Dors.   St. 5 – An.   St. 4 – Dors.–lat.

(b) 3–7 h

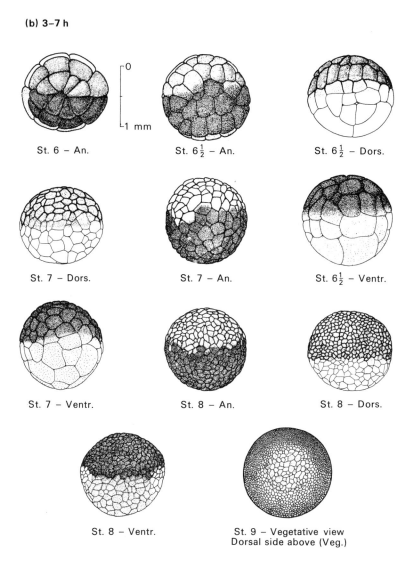

St. 6 – An.   St. 6½ – An.   St. 6½ – Dors.

St. 7 – Dors.   St. 7 – An.   St. 6½ – Ventr.

St. 7 – Ventr.   St. 8 – An.   St. 8 – Dors.

St. 8 – Ventr.   St. 9 – Vegetative view
                     Dorsal side above (Veg.)

Fig. 2

Stages in the development of *Xenopus* from the fertilised egg to the young metamorphosed tadpole. The age at which embryos and larvae reach various stages is
approximate only and relates to animals being reared under laboratory conditions at
22-24°C. (Reproduced with permission from Nieuwkoop & Faber and the North
Holland Publishing Co.).

(c) 9–17½ h

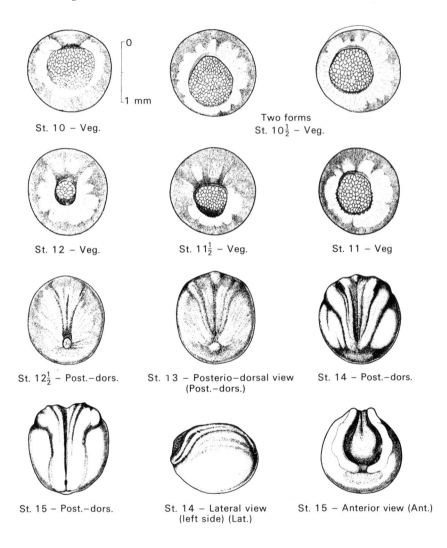

St. 10 – Veg.

0
1 mm

Two forms
St. 10½ – Veg.

St. 12 – Veg.

St. 11½ – Veg.

St. 11 – Veg

St. 12½ – Post.–dors.

St. 13 – Posterio–dorsal view
(Post.–dors.)

St. 14 – Post.–dors.

St. 15 – Post.–dors.

St. 14 – Lateral view
(left side) (Lat.)

St. 15 – Anterior view (Ant.)

(d) 18$\frac{1}{4}$ h – 1 dy 5$\frac{1}{2}$ h

St. 16 – Post.–dors.   St.20 – Dors.   St. 22 – Dors.

St. 22 – Lat.

St. 26 – Lat.

(e) $1\frac{1}{2}$ dy – $5\frac{1}{2}$ dy

St. 29/30 – Lat.   St. 33/34 – Lat.   St. 40 – Lat.
(Small ind.)

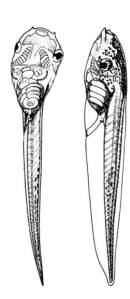

St. 47 – Ventr.   St. 47 – Lat.

(f) 7½ dy – 26 dy

Hind limbs

St. 48   St. 49   St. 50   St. 51   St. 52   St. 53   St. 54

41–54 dy

   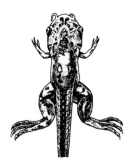

⌐0
├10
└20 mm

    St. 57 – Lat.   St. 59 – Lat.   St. 61 – Dors.

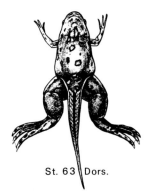 

    St. 63 – Dors.   St. 65 – Dors.

I do not want the reader to feel that this is yet another book on embryology or developmental biology. I hope that he will want to relive the excitement of investigating the varying aspects of the development of *one* animal. He can concentrate on the importance of the nucleus or the grey crescent in this one species and then see that the same animal can and does afford the answers to questions related to much later events in development.

I have tried to write the book in an enquiring manner and have been concerned with posing questions like the following:

How far is the pattern of the tadpole laid down in the fertilised egg?

How does the zygote (fertilisation) nucleus exert control over a volume of cytoplasm thousands of times greater than that of a normal cell?

What is the significance of cell movement during development? What makes an eye? How is the heart formed?

Some of these questions are not answered explicitly in the text so the reader will have to make up his own mind. Other questions posed in the text may be waiting for the reader himself to discover the answer.

A study of *Xenopus* development will undoubtedly stimulate many enquiries and investigations, to the end that the mosaic of developmental processes involved will present a clear picture of the way in which a fertilised egg can develop smoothly into a mature animal. The same problems of development are met throughout the vertebrates and their solution in *Xenopus* may be taken as a model for development.

General References

Brown, A L (1970). *The African Clawed Toad*. London: Butterworths.

Deuchar, E M (1972). *Xenopus laevis* and developmental biology. *Biol. Rev.* **47**, 37–112.

Nieuwkoop, P D & Faber, J (1956 & 1967). Normal Table of *Xenopus laevis* (Daudin). Amsterdam: North Holland Publishing Company.

1 *The Gametes*

IT is becoming increasingly apparent from studies of the biochemistry of amphibian embryos that substances laid down in the oocyte are of paramount importance to the early development of the embryo.

When it is laid, the *Xenopus* egg contains sufficient stored materials to allow the embryo to develop for four days at 23°C. Only at this age does the young tadpole start feeding.

What is stored in the egg and how does it differ from the male gamete, the sperm?

During the development of both egg and sperm the nucleus undergoes two meiotic divisions, at the first of which there is a prolonged prophase during which pairing of chromosomes and crossing over take place. At the end of the first meiotic division the nuclei *become haploid* and at the end of the second meiotic division the chromosomes are reduced to chromatids.

The haploid male cells then *lose* much of their cytoplasm and develop a propulsive flagellary tail before becoming sperm.

During the development of the egg on the other hand, the volume of the egg cytoplasm increases greatly and growth ceases *before* the end of the first meiotic division.

In the egg, therefore, cytoplasmic maturity precedes nuclear maturity, whereas in the sperm it succeeds nuclear maturity.

Oogenesis

While the oocyte is still in the prophase of the first meiotic division two types of substance are being stored. The first, RNA, is of nuclear origin; the second of maternal origin is built up into yolk platelets.

1 *Nuclear activity*
Although the nucleus has to undergo a meiotic division to attain the haploid number of chromosomes, the growth phase of the oocyte is almost

entirely passed during the protracted prophase of the first meiotic division. The nucleus becomes a large clear sac called the germinal vesicle which can be removed entire from the developing oocyte. If such a germinal vesicle is squashed and stained it can be seen to contain long frilly chromosomes, reminiscent of lamp brushes to the nineteenth century cytologists. Nowadays we still call the germinal vesicle chromosomes, lampbrush chromosomes. Chiasmata may be seen between them.

Lampbrush chromosomes are very active in RNA synthesis and at the beginning of oocyte growth are known to be the site of transfer RNA[1] synthesis. As the oocytes increase in size by the deposition of yolk in the cytoplasm, so the nuclear RNA synthesis switches more to the production of ribosomal RNA[2]. The massive synthesis of ribosomes, which in the mature egg will be adequate for the embryo's needs for two days, is accomplished in the following manner.

It appears that the segments of DNA which are responsible for the synthesis of ribosomal RNA are replicated about fifteen-thousand fold and break away from the chromosomes to become associated with the fifteen thousand or so, satellite nucleoli visible in the germinal vesicle[3]. Enormous numbers of ribosomes are thus made in the large oocyte without involving the replication or continued activity of the whole genome.

Throughout oogenesis the synthesis of messenger RNA (template or DNA-like RNA) continues at a slow rate. About 2–3 per cent of the lampbrush chromosome DNA actively produces mRNA which is retained throughout oogenesis[4]. By the end of oogenesis it amounts to almost 4000 times the total amount of chromosomal DNA in the oocyte nucleus, and is still present in the mature oocyte.

2 *Cytoplasmic or maternal activity*

The synthesis of yolk has also been a subject of recent study and it has been confirmed that substances are released by the liver of female *Xenopus* which are quickly incorporated into oocytes. These substances must enter oocytes through the follicle cells via the macrovilli and microvilli on the cells' surfaces and are then made up into yolk platelets (Fig. 3). It is possible too that DNA from degenerating liver nuclei are incorporated into yolk platelets[5].

It has been demonstrated that, while most of the small oocytes' mitochondria are aggregated in the centre of the cell, a few mitochondria lie subcortically[6]. The latter seem to be transformed into yolk platelets by acting as crystallisation centres for the yolk lipoproteins[7]. Later in oocyte development, when the cells reach a diameter of about 300μm there is an indication that pigment granules may also arise from modified sub-cortical mitochondria. Meanwhile the mass of mitochondria located near the nucleus has proliferated enormously. It then gradually moves towards the outer layers of the oocyte and breaks up[7].

Streams of mitochondria on their way to the oocyte cortex pass streams of yolk platelets moving into deeper regions. Cortical granules also pass to the surface from the Golgi apparatus.

The relationship between the oocyte and a follicle cell is shown in Fig. 3 as are the sites of synthesis of various cytoplasmic organelles during synthesis and after ovulation.

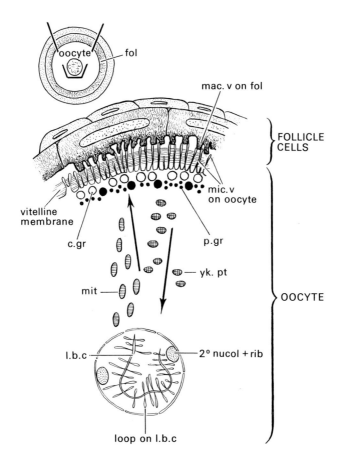

Fig. 3
Diagram of the developing oocyte and its relationship with the surrounding follicle cells. (Based on Balinsky & Devis[7] and other authors).

3 *Maturation*

The final stages of oocyte development, including the dissolution of the germinal vesicle, are stimulated by pituitary gonadotrophins. These may be natural or of mammalian origin[8]. If mammalian hormone is injected into a female *Xenopus* the germinal vesicles of full-grown oocytes disrupt, disgorging their contents into the cytoplasm. The chromosomes condense and pass to the pigmented pole of the oocyte to complete the first meiotic division. Although the daughter nuclei are equivalent, the accompanying cytoplasmic division is extremely unequal. One nucleus remains in the oocyte which has a diameter of about 1·3mm while the other passes to the first polar body with a diameter of about 10μm.

The oocyte still surrounded by the vitelline membrane, is now liberated from the ovary and on its passage through the female's enlarged oviduct is coated with several layers of jelly on top of the vitelline membrane. At this time the microvillous projections can be seen as mere stubs on the cortex.

By the time the eggs are released from the body of the female, which is normally 8–18 hours after hormone injection, the nucleus is at metaphase of the second meiotic division. It will not complete this division until the egg has been fertilised or activated in some other way.

References

1 Mairy, M & Denis, H (1971). Recherches biochimiques sur l'oogenèse 1. Synthèse et accumulation du RNA pendant l'oogenèse du crapaud sud-africain *Xenopus laevis. Develop. Biol.* **24,** 143–65.

2 Brown, D D & Littna, E (1964). Variations in the synthesis of stable RNA during oogenesis and development of *Xenopus laevis. J. Mol. Biol.* **8,** 688–95.

3 Evans, D & Birnstiel, M L (1968). Localisation of amplified ribosomal DNA in the oöcyte of *Xenopus laevis. Biochim. Biophys. Acta* **166,** 274–6.

4 Davidson, E H, Crippa, M, Kramer, F R & Mirsky, A E (1966). Genomic function during the lampbrush chromosome stage of of amphibian oögenesis. *Proc. Natl. Acad. Sci.* Wash. **56,** 856–63.

5 Wallace, R A, Jared, D W & Nelson, B L (1970). Protein incorporation by isolated amphibian oocytes 1. Preliminary studies. *J. exp. Zool.* **175,** 259–70.

6 Al-Mukhtar, K A K & Webb, A C (1971). An ultra-structural study of primordial germ cells, oogonia and early oocytes in *Xenopus laevis*. *J. Embryol. exp. Morph.* **26,** 195–217.

7 Balinski, B I & Devis, R J (1963). Origin and differentiation of cytoplasmic structures in the oocytes of *Xenopus laevis*. *Acta Embryol. Morph. exp.* **6,** 55–108.

8 Detlaff, T A, Nikitina, L A & Stroeva, O G (1964). The role of the germinal vesicle in oocyte maturation in anurans as revealed by removal and transplantation of nuclei. *J. Embryol. exp. Morph.* **12,** 851–73.

2 *Initial Development of the Embryo*

Fertilisation

THE male partner to an ovulating female grips her around the waist (amplexus) and when he feels her laying eggs he releases sperm. The relative positions of the male and female ensure that sperm reach the eggs as soon as the eggs are expelled by the female. One of the sperm released will penetrate each fertilised egg.

Many changes in the arrangement of the contents of the unfertilised egg take place on fertilisation. Firstly, the vitelline membrane is raised by the expulsion of cortical granules which causes a space to form between the egg and its outer membranes[9]. Within the egg the large yolk platelets move from a vegetal pole location deeper into the interior, while the middle-sized and small yolk platelets move down the sides of the embryo to take up space vacated by some of the largest platelets.

During this shift in egg contents the pigment granules, which remain in the cortex of the animal hemisphere, appear to contract towards the pole and, as observed in sections form a smaller cap of a thicker layer of pigment. About 15 minutes after fertilisation the pigment collapses back to cover a larger area more sparsely, but this time the pigment on one side drops further than that on the other side forming the grey crescent. In this way the original radial symmetry of the egg has been changed to bilateral. The left/right axis bisects the grey crescent which has appeared as a result of the uneven return of the pigment cap, and coincides with the point of sperm entry which is diametrically opposite the widest part of the grey crescent.

The question of the ultimate determination of the plane of bilateral symmetry hinges on whether the point of sperm penetration is in some way predetermined by egg structure or whether the sperm enters at a random position and does itself determine the symmetry of the fertilised egg.

The reason why the grey crescent has been discussed is because it is particularly important in the future development of the egg. It is known to become the 'organising' region of the embryo (see gastrulation); but whereas it was shown 50 years ago by Spemann and Mangold[10] that cells grafted from this region of one gastrula into an ectopic region of another could induce a secondary embryo to develop, there has until recently been no proof that such a quality existed in the grey crescent of an uncleaved egg.

In experiments, making exquisite use of the observation that the *Xenopus* egg cortex could be loosened from the main mass of the egg by removing all calcium and magnesium from the medium[11], pieces of cortex from one egg could be cut out and placed anywhere on the surface of another egg and sealed in place by the replacement of calcium and magnesium in excess. If the cortex from the grey crescent, and grey crescent only was placed away from the host's own grey crescent, it later developed into the 'organiser' of a second embryo. The processes involved will be discussed later under gastrulation.

These initial events after fertilisation largely concern the cytoplasm but the gamete nuclei are also involved in changes leading up to the time at which they fuse. The egg nucleus is arrested at metaphase of the second meiotic division from soon after ovulation until fertilisation when the egg receives the stimulus to complete that division. At this meiotic division again the division of the cytoplasm is unequal giving rise to another polar body whose only function appears to be that of containing cast-off chromosomes. At 20°C the extrusion of the second polar body is completed 20 minutes after fertilisation[12]. The egg nucleus and the sperm nucleus then swell and move inward towards each other. They incorporate tritiated thymidine actively, indicating that they are synthesising DNA. Forty minutes after fertilisation, the pronuclei lie side by side in the animal hemisphere but it is not until about 10 minutes later that the nuclear membranes break down and the zygote (or embryonic) nucleus enters the first mitosis. Telophase of the first division is reached and the first sign of first cleavage is evident 70 minutes after fertilisation.

Cleavage

The first cleavage normally bisects the grey crescent as it passes down the egg from animal pole to vegetal pole so that the two initial cells, or blastomeres represent the left and right sides of the embryo. The next division is at right angles to the first and gives rise to four blastomeres, each of which contains both animal and vegetal material. These four blastomeres then divide equatorially and unequally into animal pole and vegetal pole cells, that is, into pigmented slightly yolky cells and unpigmented heavily yolked cells. At this time an internal cavity is clearly visible, surrounded by the rounded corners of the first eight blastomeres.

After the first three cleavages the synchrony of division breaks down in that the animal pole cells are in advance of the vegetal pole cells. Among themselves the animal and vegetal cells divide synchronously for another three or four divisions, maintaining the very rapid rate of 20 minutes per cell cycle.

Biochemical studies indicate that the rapid rate of cell division is only possible because of the store of easily accessible precursors of DNA and protein that were laid down in oogenesis. The embryonic cells do not have to grow between divisions neither do the nuclei have to be the site of RNA synthesis. It has not been possible to detect RNA synthesis during cleavage stages but the nuclei are engaged in a cycle of DNA synthesis and mitosis[12]. A lack of RNA synthesis does not mean that there is no protein synthesis, for the cells would be unable to divide without new proteins for the increasing numbers of cell membranes and mitotic apparatus.

In order to determine the importance of the various steps between the DNA instructions and the final protein, embryos have been treated with substances that are known to interfere at specific places in the chain.

Experimental studies have shown that substances which prevent the synthesis of messenger RNA (e.g. Actinomycin D) have no effect on the process of cleavage. On the other hand, cleavage can be arrested and protein synthesis in general brought to a halt by treatment with puromycin. Puromycin is known not to affect the synthesis of mRNA so much as the reading of the message[13].

Ultrastructural studies of cleavage and blastocoel formation

Changes in the pigmentation of the animal pole herald the onset of first cleavage. These have been described many times for different amphibia. The ultrastructural changes at the surface of an egg which is about to cleave for the first time have been studied in the axolotl. *Xenopus* cleavage follows the same course closely so that a description of the inception of cleavage in the axolotl will be given here[14], but it will be illustrated with E. M. pictures of *Xenopus*.

These electron microscope studies have shown that, within the region of the initial surface changes in pigmentation that anticipate cleavage, the cortex of the egg is thrown into folds (Fig. 4a). As a shallow depression

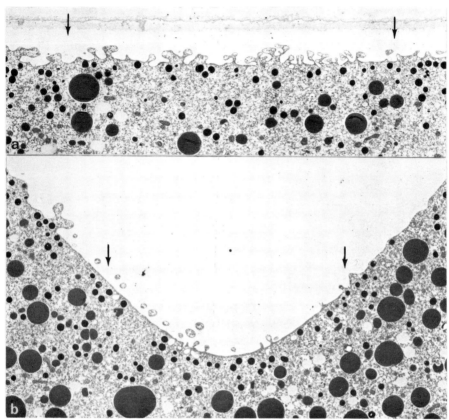

Fig. 4 Progression of the first cleavage furrow from the SS-stage (single stripe) to the SG-stage (shallow groove). At the SS-stage (a) the zygote surface is thrown into folds in the region of the stripe (between the arrows). By the SG-stage (b), about four minutes later, the surface has indented and there are no longer long surface projections. Both × 3800. (with grateful thanks to Dr J G Bluemink).

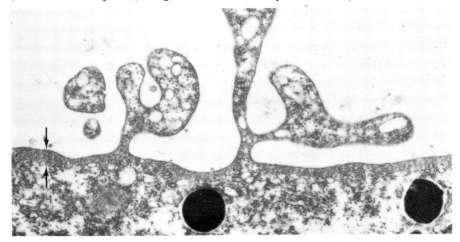

Fig. 5 Enlargement of the single stripe region showing the oriented microfilaments in cross-section. They form a $0.1 - 0.15$ μm thick layer which is 20–24μm wide by the SG-stage × 21 000. (By courtesy of Dr J G Bluemink).

deepens into a 'U' shaped groove (4b) so the projections from the cortex become longer at the edge of the groove, but are pulled into longitudinal ridges along the centre and bottom of the trough. Microfilaments (Fig. 5) which are characteristic of cell motility appear indicating the sites of cleavage furrow contraction. The microfilaments act rather like a draw-string just under the surface of the animal pole which throws the cortex at the side of the furrow into folds which are visible with a dissecting micro-scope. The initial development of the first furrow appears to be confined to the animal pole whence it spreads inwards and round the circumference of the egg (Fig. 6). As the first cleavage furrow penetrates into the depth of the egg, so we return to a description of the development of *Xenopus*.

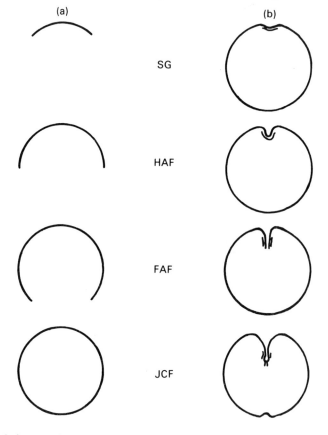

Fig. 6

Diagram of cleavage furrow progression showing (a) the extent to which the furrow has progressed externally and (b) the depth to which the furrow has penetrated the egg. The location of microfilaments is indicated by the short line adjacent to the furrow in (b).

SG shallow groove, HAF half advanced furrow, FAF far advanced furrow, JCF just completed furrow.

Stages based on external criteria (after Dr J. G Bluemink).

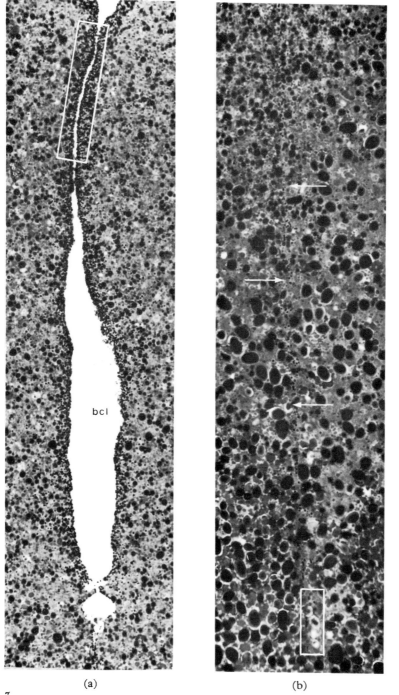

(a)   (b)

Fig. 7

(a) and (b) together form a light micrograph of a long, but as yet incomplete first cleavage furrow. (a) is the most 'animal' part, and the region above the incipient blastocoel (bcl) is closed from the exterior by the close apposition of the two sides in the boxed area. (b) beneath the blastocoel the furrow can be made out by the line of pigment granules. The furrow ends in the box. × 740.
(By courtesy of Dr M Kalt [15] and the Company of Biologists.)

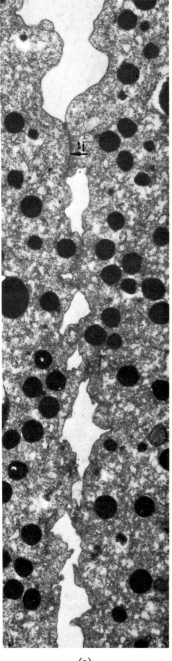
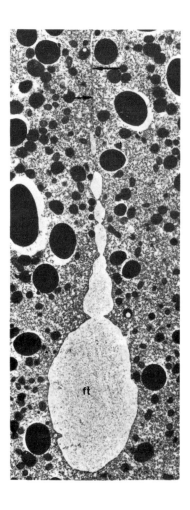

Fig. 8   (a)   (b)

(a) Electron micrograph of an area similar to the box in Fig. 7 (a). There are tight junctions (t.j.) where the two sides of the furrow have come together. × 7 600. (b) The most vegetal region of an animal pole furrow which has not yet met the vegetal furrow. The furrow tip (f.t.) is dilated. × 3 000. (From Dr M Kalt[15] in *Journal of Embryology and Experimental Morphology*, by courtesy of the Company of Biologists).

The U-shaped groove becomes deeper and the edges of the furrow, near the surface of the egg, come together closing off the widened region within the egg[15] (Fig. 6 JCF). The area of contact is so close that the enclosed cavity loses its connection with the outside (Fig. 7a and 8a) and is enlarged by the disgorgement of glycogen from the neighbouring regions of the first two blastomeres. Further downgrowth of the animal pole furrow below the level of the equator, proceeds by the simple addition of new cell membranes between the separating blastomeres (Fig. 7b and 8b). The blastocoel rudiment remains within the animal half of the embryo. The final extension of the animal pole furrow is met by the U-shaped vegetal pole furrow to complete the first cleavage.

The first signs of first cleavage that were visible as changes in the cortex had been preceded by a massive advance spread of ectoplasm which settled in the region of the future blastocoel. There is no such movement of ectoplasm associated with the second cleavage furrow. Much of the pathway of the second cleavage is through ectoplasmic regions of the embryo since it also passes from the animal to vegetal poles, but it is at right angles to the first cleavage. In transverse sections it can be seen that the second furrow passes through the first two blastomeres forming close junctions as it proceeds and is not swollen at the tip like the first one. The ectoplasm is undisturbed.

The next cleavages of the embryo are initiated in the rich ectoplasmic region located *in the middle* of the egg, not in the surface cortex. This means that, although cleavage furrows can still be seen on the outside of the embryo they are first apparent interiorly. Close junctions are spaced away from the blastocoel, so the new cell membranes situated between blastocoel and the nearest junction become part of the blastocoel wall. The blastocoel continues to expand by the accumulation of glycogen. The external portion of each furrow, accompanied by a slight ectoplasmic zone, forms tight junctions along its length.

By about the sixth cleavage there is almost no difference between the two ends of a new furrow and the blastocoel ceases to grow by the addition of furrow material. The impermeability of the junctions between cells at the blastula stage has been demonstrated by injecting a fluorescent dye into one cell[16]. The dye did not diffuse into neighbouring cells, but remained in the one cell and its progeny (Fig. 9).

The blastocoel continues to enlarge throughout the rest of the blastula stage by the intake of water and becomes more and more displaced towards the animal side of the embryo. It is surrounded on the upper surface by a double layer of small cells and underneath by large yolky cells, a few deep.

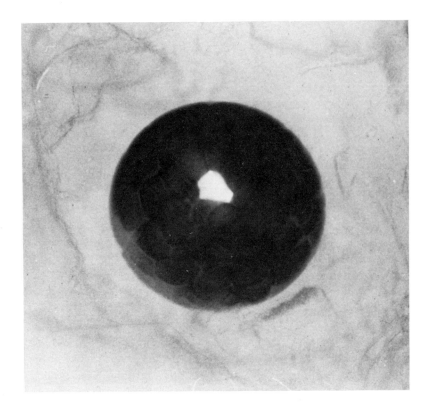

Fig 9
Photograph of a blastula with one cell brightly labelled with fluorescene. (By courtesy of Drs Slack and Palmer,[16] and Academic Press who publish *Experimental Cell Research*).

In the later stages of the blastula the animal pole cells begin to move relative to the vegetal cells. As the animal cells spread down the lower surface of the embryo, so the vegetal cells, or future endoderm, are pushed into the interior of the embryo. The blastocoel is no longer confined to the animal hemisphere, but is extended down the sides of the embryo by the upward and inward shift of the endoderm and the downward spread of the animal pole cells (Fig. 10a).

At this time there is evidence that transfer and messenger RNA are being synthesised *de novo*, however, the embryo does not rely on them until the next stage, gastrulation, begins[17].

References

9   Balinsky, B I (1966). Changes in the ultrastructure of amphibian eggs following fertilisation. *Acta Embryol. Morph. exp.* **9,** 132–54.

10 Spemann, H (1938). *Embryonic development and induction.* Ch. VII. Induction of a secondary embryo by an 'organiser'. Yale University Press. Reprinted 1962 by Hafner Publishing Co. Inc. New York 3.

11 Curtis, A S G (1960). Cortical grafting in *Xenopus laevis. J. Embryol. exp. Morph.* **8,** 163–73.

12 Graham, C F (1966). The regulation of DNA synthesis and mitosis in multinucleate frog eggs. *J. Cell Sci.* **1,** 363–74.

13 Brachet, J, Denis, H & de Vitry, F (1964). The effects of actinomycin D and puromycin on morphogenesis in amphibian eggs and *Acetabularia mediterranea. Develop. Biol.* **9,** 398–'434.

14 Bluemink, J G (1970). The first cleavage of the amphibian egg. An electron microscopic study of the onset of cytokinesis in the egg of *Ambystoma mexicanum. J. Ultrastructure Research.* **32,** 142–66.

15 Kalt, M R (1971). The relationship between cleavage and blastocoel formation in *Xenopus laevis* II. Electron microscopic observations. *J. Embryol. exp. Morph.* **26,** 51–66.

16 Slack, C & Palmer, J F (1969). The permeability of intercellular junctions in the early embryo of *Xenopus laevis,* studied with a fluorescent tracer. *Exp. Cell Res.* **55,** 416–19.

17 Gurdon, J B & Woodland, H R (1969). The Influence of the cytoplasm on the nucleus during cell differentiation with special reference to RNA synthesis during amphibian cleavage. *Proc. Roy. Soc., B.* **173,** 99–111.

3 Embryo Formation — Gastrulation and Neurulation

DURING these stages the embryo begins to look more like a vertebrate for it develops an alimentary canal and a dorsal nerve cord by large scale movements of sheets of cells. Cavities and tubes are formed by migration and folding, and reach from the head to the tail of the embryo.

Gastrulation[18]

It will be remembered that in the later stages of the blastula there are signs of epiboly or overgrowth of the embryo by the future ectoderm. During gastrulation these movements are continued and exaggerated until the endoderm is contained within the embryo and completely surrounded by ectoderm (Fig. 2, stages 8–12).

Another group of cells—the mesoderm—which lie within that part of the embryo demarcated by the grey crescent and forming an equatorial portion of the blastocoel roof also moves into the interior of the embryo. However, only the underlying deep layer of the roof of the blastocoel forms the mesoderm. The deep cells at the site of the grey crescent begin to slide round the lower edge of the blastocoel and lie over the endoderm on the floor of the blastocoel. They are propelled further into the embryo when an externally visible slit appears in the endoderm close beneath the grey crescent (stage $10\frac{1}{2}$). The slit is lined with endoderm cells and increases in size by the addition of more endoderm cells that roll over the edge of the slit. The newly formed cavity, called the archenteron or primitive gut, pushes the blastocoel out of the way.

The outward sign of the slit or groove round which the mesodermal cells move internally is called the dorsal lip of the blastopore (Fig. 10b). The lips of the blastopore then extend laterally and meet ventrally so that what was once a slit is now a circle with cells invaginating at its circumference. The visible endoderm cells, surrounded by the diminishing circular blastopore, are called the yolk plug, and since they fit the surrounding lips of the blastopore tightly act as a plug for the archenteron which

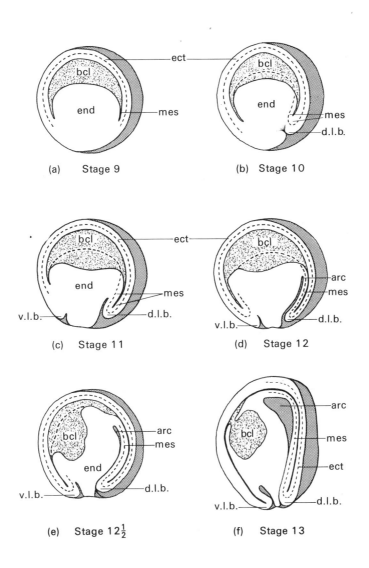

Fig. 10

Drawings of half embryos during gastrulation. During this process the mesoderm and endoderm invaginate, and a new cavity–the archenteron–develops at the expense of the blastocoel. The location of the enlarged archenteron at stage 13 causes the embryo to tip into the belly down position.

For abbreviations see p.76.

is filling with fluid (stage 11). This fluid is probably derived from the shrinking blastocoel. Now, although the external view of the embryo still gives the impression of radial symmetry there is, in fact, very strong bilateral symmetry inside the embryo for the majority of the endoderm cells roll into the interior of the embryo through the dorsal side of the yolk plug. The bulk of the yolky cells still lie as a mass within the embryo, but those endoderm cells that were superficial in the blastula have now spread out to line the whole of the archenteron. They are overlain by mesoderm on the dorsal side (Fig. 10b to f).

It will be seen that the position of the fluid filled archenteron and the mass of yolky endoderm cells make the yolk-plug-down position unstable by the end of gastrulation. The embryo then swings round to the belly-down position with head and tail in the horizontal (Fig. 10f).

Thus we see that the movements of gastrulation which are *epiboly* (overgrowth by the ectoderm), *invagination* (the passing in of the endoderm and mesoderm) and *convergence* (at the dorsal lip of the blastopore) bring cells from which the tissues of the embryo and the larva will form into their appropriate places.

The bilateral symmetry imposed on the embryo at fertilisation, now has added to it definitive dorsoventral and anteroposterior axes. Cells which were poles apart now lie in proximity in the head region.

Neurulation

The first external signs of neurulation, or neural tube formation, are three longitudinal lines of pigment along the dorsal surface of the late gastrula embryo. They represent the mid-dorsal line and the lateral limits of the neural plate. (See Fig. 2, stage 13,). Soon two other more lateral lines become visible and together with the previously marked out lateral lines delimit the neural folds. The neural folds are elevated long-itudinal ridges which rise above the rest of the embryo's dorsal surface and move towards the dorsal midline. The neural plate is wider and the neural folds deeper on the anterior surface of the embryo where the forebrain develops. The neural folds come into contact with each other simultaneously along their length except for the most anterior and posterior portions. These regions close together rather more slowly, but even so, there is no sign of the junction after a few hours, for once again, the dorsal ectoderm forms an intact sheet.

In section, one can see the cell reorganisation taking place during the formation of the neural tube[19]. It will be remembered from the description

of the ectoderm at the beginning of gastrulation that it may be sub-
divided into two layers—the superficial and the deep or sensorial. In
Xenopus both these layers contribute to the formation of the neural tube
and both are to be found in the neural fold. When the folds come together,
the most lateral cells of the neural plate become the most medial and dorsal.
It appears that the superficial cells that remain on the outside of the
embryo will not unite across the midline unless they are severed from the
superficial cells that line the neural tube. This is accomplished when the
now most dorsal cells of the deep layer move into the midline. The
distinction between cells derived from deep and superficial layers disappears within the neural tube when they interdigitate to form a single
layer of cells around the neural canal. The process of neural fold closure
is shown in Fig. 11.

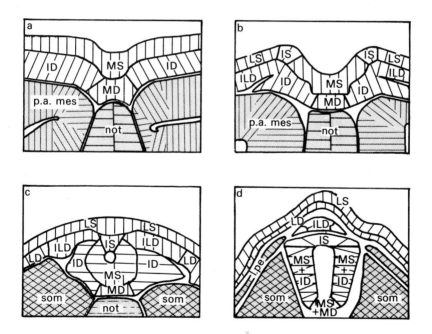

Fig. 11
The development of the neural tube from both superficial and deep layers of the
ectoderm. The orientation of the cells is indicated. Mesodermal structures are shaded,
the ectodermal ones are not.
(a) stage 13, (b) stage 16, (c) stage 20, (d) stage 22.
D = deep; I = intermediate; L = lateral; M = median; S = superficial.
For other abbreviations see p. 76. (After Schroeder[19]).

Induction

It can be seen from Fig. 11 that the neural ectoderm and underlying mesoderm are in close aposition throughout most of neurulation, and indeed, they were increasingly so during gastrulation. It is now known that this close proximity between ectoderm and mesoderm is essential at the very beginning of gastrulation if a normal neural tube is to develop. In fact, if an operation is performed to transplant early dorsal lip material from one embryo into a ventrally equivalent position on another embryo, two sites of invagination will appear and later, two neural tubes[20] (Fig. 12).

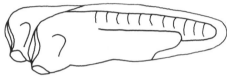

Fig. 12
Two headed embryo produced by grafting an additional dorsal lip at stage 10. (After Cooke[20]).

If such an operation is performed with slightly older dorsal lips, the secondary embryo may lack some head structures. It has been concluded from this type of experiment that the mesoderm that invaginates round the dorsal lip of the blastopore can *induce* the ectoderm, under which it comes to lie, to form neural tissue. In the best of cases, where it induces the formation of a complete secondary embryo, a very early dorsal lip was transplanted. It was shown to cause the local ectoderm to invaginate and become mesodermal-like in behaviour. Thus the greater the size of the mesodermal mantle, the more neural tissue is induced.

The dramatic developmental powers shown by grafted dorsal lips of the blastopore of newts led the great experimental embryologist of the 1920's, H Spemann, to call them the primary organiser in amphibian development.

There are, of course, questions that are raised by such findings and three of them can be considered here since it is possible to perform the appropriate operations in the class room. (Appendix 2a, b and c, p. 70)

    1. Can the surface of the blastula be mapped out to find the destination of the cells at the late neurula stage?

    2. What happens to the ectoderm and mesoderm if they can be prevented from coming in contact during gastrulation?

    3. What happens if an early dorsal lip is implanted into the blastocoel of an early gastrula and comes in contact with the ectoderm that way?

In order to answer these questions yourselves, it is essential to use absolutely clean equipment and keep your own hands clean because in every case the outer jellies and the vitelline membrane have to be removed. The embryos are also very fragile and rather cheesy in texture.

1. The outside of the embryo can be stained with non-poisonous 'vital' dyes which impregnate groups of cells but will not diffuse out again. Several dyes can be used and if their positions are recorded, a picture can be built up of which cells go where during gastrulation. In the 1920's Vogt developed such a technique and it was used extensively to build up fate maps for the surface cells of amphibian blastulae (Fig. 13). This fate map is that derived for a generalised Anuran.

Unfortunately, for this study, *Xenopus* is aberrant in having no meso-dermal cells in the superficial layer of the late blastula. However, ecto- and endodermal cells can be vitally stained to show the fate of these cells at the end of gastrulation and neurulation.

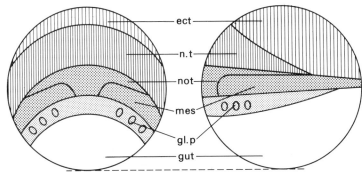

Fig. 13
Presumptive regions of a generalised frog such as can be mapped out using Vogt's technique. For abbreviations see p. 76.

2. As we have seen the fate of the ectodermal cells may be modified by the presence of underlying mesoderm. We can also demonstrate that pro-spective neural tissue requires mesoderm in order to form neural struc-tures. In this experiment a naked late blastula is reared in a solution hypertonic to its cell contents in order to produce an exogastrula; in other amphibia an isotonic solution is adequate. As the word suggests an exogastrula is one in which those tissues which should invaginate, evag-inate instead. The result is an embryo in which there is no archenteron since both endoderm and mesoderm have moved away from the ectoderm which has expanded and thinned as it would normally have done. The rather floppy bag of ectoderm shows no sign of neural development, and thus answers part of the question relating to the development of isolated ectoderm.

The mesoderm on the other hand, seems to develop autonomously and many mesodermal structures can be identified in older exogastrulae.

3. Dorsal lip that is implanted into the blastocoel of an early gastrula, will become pressed up against the host's ectoderm as the blastocoel is reduced in size during gastrulation. If the implant is placed on the side opposite the host's dorsal lip, then it will come to lie under belly ectoderm. In such a position, it can and does exert an inducing influence upon the ectoderm.

In conclusion, it may be said that, by knowing the position of the grey crescent, the movements of the mesoderm during gastrulation may be predicted. Since the final position of the mesodermal mantle is known, the position of the neural plate is also known, for the one induces the other.

The mesodermal cells have rightly been called the primary organiser.

References

18 Nieuwkoop, P D & Florschütz, P (1950). Quelques caractères spéciaux de la gastrulation et de la neurulation de l'oeuf de *X. laevis* et de quelques autres Anoures 1. Etude descriptive. *Arch. Biol. (Liège)* **61,** 113–50.

19 Schroeder, T E (1970). Neurulation in *Xenopus laevis*. An analysis and model based upon light and electron microscopy. *J. Embryol. exp. Morph.* **23,** 427–62.

20 Cooke, J (1972). Properties of the primary organization field in the embryo of *Xenopus laevis* II. Positional information for axial organisation in embryos with two head organisers. *J. Embryol. exp. Morph.* **28,** 27–46.

4 *Further Development of the Embryo*

THE process of neurulation is the last phase of the embryo's development that can conveniently be discussed within the 'whole embryo'
context for thereafter the total description of the embryo's development
becomes too cumbersome. It is for this reason that the description of the
development of the embryo will be sub-divided into convenient regions.
These regions fall naturally into the following three groups:

1. central nervous system and other derivatives of the neural plate,
   which will be discussed in this chapter.
2. mesodermal tissues (described in Chapter 5), and
3. endodermal tissues (see Chapter 6).

Neural plate derivatives

Brain and neural tube

Closure of the neural tube has been described in Chapter 3 and the
newly formed neural tube has to differentiate subsequently into the
intricately co-ordinated brain and spinal cord. Very little is known about
the determination and fate of the individual cells lying within these
structures, but between them they make up the communications network
in the body.

During its development the brain is divided into three gross regions
which are called the fore-, mid- and hind-brain. These enlargements are
each associated with one of the three pairs of organs of special sense. The
fore-brain sends fibres directly to the olfactory organs (smell) and is
usually bifurcated for this reason. The eyes although they grow out of the
forebrain, become functionally associated with the mid-brain (this part of
the brain also being associated with the pituitary and pineal bodies) while
the most posterior part of the brain, the hind-brain, is functionally
linked to the ear and lateral line system (vibration and posture).

Throughout the central nervous system co-ordinated impulses have to
be sent to and received from the periphery.

The nerves connecting the central nervous system with the periphery are of two sorts i.e. efferent and afferent, and they have a different origin and arrangement from each other. The former develop from cells which lie within the spinal cord and send projections out to the somites and viscera. Their segmentation is determined by the somites which receive one nerve (collection of fibres) at the middle of their length. The second sort of nerve fibre (afferent) is derived from neural crest cells which settle near the dorsal surface of the neural tube and brain. The cells remain outside the neural tube but send short axons into the tube and longer ones to peripheral sites, both visceral and somatic. The collections of sensory nerve cell bodies are grouped at intervals to form dorsal root ganglia and are arranged *between* the somites. It appears that the positions of the somites are responsible for the placing of the dorsal roots for it has been shown that if somites are added or subtracted during tail bud stages the number and location of dorsal root ganglia is modified accordingly.

When the vertebrae develop there is no longer space for sensory nerves to pass out between the somites (myotomes) so the nerves are pushed forwards instead and emerge between the vertebrae together with the appropriate motor nerve. This is why the sensory component of a mixed nerve has a more posterior origin than the motor nerve with which it is paired.

In returning our attention to the brain it is possible to assign the cranial nerves to a segmented arrangement. The somitic motor nerves are not part of the large mixed nerves here, as can be seen with cranial nerves III, IV, and VI. The muscles innervated by these nerves are the eye muscles, and although the origin of these muscles in *Xenopus* is not *obviously* somitic as it is in some cartilaginous fish, it is presumed to be so.

The remaining innervation of the head is made up of sensory (neural crest) and visceral motor nerves which connect the brain with the musculature of the visceral skeleton.

The origin of the peripheral nervous system is well known. Although only the sensory nerves are derived from the neural crest *all* nerve axons lying outside the central nervous system are sheathed with insulating Schwann cells (i.e. they are myelinated), themselves derived from the neural crest.

Cells within the central nervous system, are also myelinated, but by cells of neural tube origin. Most of the long axons within the spinal cord are passing impulses to and from the brain but there are also important connections between segments. In the brain the situation is more complicated because the nerves branch and communicate with the areas of the brain associated with the organs of special sense.

The *pituitary gland* develops as an outgrowth of the posterior part of the mid-brain and owes its complete structure to a contribution from the ectoderm. The infundibulum or pars nervosa is a blind sac-like extension of the ventral part of the brain immediately in front of the tip of the notochord. In its downward growth it is met by cells moving backwards from the ectoderm above the mouth. They form a discrete column of cells so that their removal from a tail-bud embryo is fairly simple and an embryo lacking the hypophysis is the result.

Soon after the hypophysis comes in contact with the infundibulum the stalk connecting it with the ectoderm disintegrates. The close relationship of the hypophysis with the infundibulum and the brain persists for life and is essential for the proper working of many dependent endocrine glands.

The eye
The eye is an organ which develops as a specialisation of the posterior forebrain—at least in so far as the retina is concerned. In common with many other developmental processes so far described, its formation is by folding of pre-existing sheets of cells.

The newly formed brain is wide in the position of the developing forebrain and its lateral walls protrude like small balloons. These become the neural elements of the eye and are called the optic vesicles. (Fig. 14). The optic vesicles grow out so far that they touch the overlying ecto-

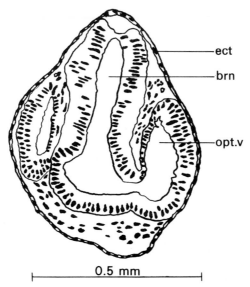

ect

brn

opt.v

0.5 mm

Fig. 14
Camera lucida drawing through the forebrain and optic vesicles at the beginning of eye development (Stage 25/26). For abbreviations see p. 76.

derm. In amphibian species, other than *Xenopus*, it is known that close contact between the optic vesicles and ectoderm is important in the transformation of some ectodermal cells into lenses by induction. In *Xenopus* it appears that after removal of the optic vesicles lenses will still develop, so perhaps induction is less important here.

The brief contact of the optic vesicles with the overlying ectoderm is followed by a collapse of the walls of the optic vesicles to form an optic cup which is attached to the brain by a relatively narrow optic stalk. The cup is formed by the collapse of those cells which are continuous with the floor of the brain into those which are continuous with the sides of the brain (Fig. 15). This sounds, at best, as though the eye cannot be more

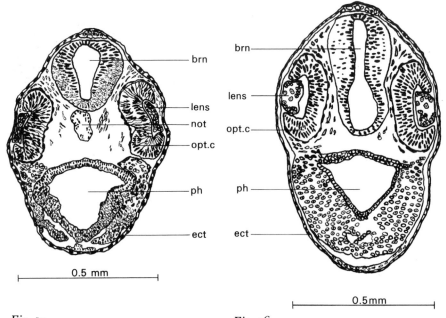

Fig. 15
Further development of the eye at stage 29 (ćamera lucida). For abbreviations see p. 76.

Fig. 16
Three layers of cells are visible in the sensory retina and the lens is enlarging at stage 33 (ćamera lucida).

than hemispherical, however, the sides of the collapsing optic vesicle expand ventrally and close together round the optic stalk. Even before the optic vesicles become the optic cup there is an observable difference in the arrangements of the cells which will lie on the outside and inside of the optic cup. The outer cells make up a very thin epithelium which becomes heavily pigmented while in the inner layer the cells are tall and closely packed. At first this inner layer is a simple, thick columnar epithelium like most of the early central nervous system. Later it becomes three-layered (Fig. 16), but still keeps the cellular arrangement characteristic of the central nervous system. This means that the cell bodies lie on the inside and nerve fibres on the outside. When referred back to the eye, it means that the light passing to the photosensitive retinal cells has to traverse the nerve fibres and ganglion cells before it can be sensed. Hence the term 'inverted retina' to describe the vertebrate eye.

During its growth the edges of the optic cup keep in close contact with the overlying ectoderm and its derivative, the lens. So much so that when the cup was forming the lens seemed almost to be dragged into the eye cavity. In any case, the outermost edges of the eye cup fold over between the lens and the ectoderm. These edges of the sensory retina and pigmented epithelium together form the iris and do not contain any active photoreceptor cells (Fig. 17a and b).

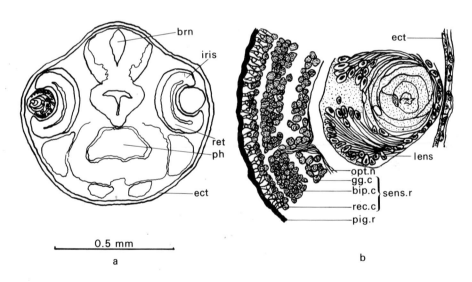

Fig. 17
The retina and the lens are now well formed and are easily recognised (camera lucida) (a) outline of whole section, (b) detail of lens and retina. For abbreviations see p. 76.

The photosensitive cells are situated at the back of the eye and appear to take no part in growth of the eye. At all stages of growth, whether tadpole or frog, mitoses are only observed at the iris margin[21]. The eye cup grows more extensively from the dorsal margins than from the ventral with the result that what was the 'centre' of the retina in the young tadpole has been shifted to ventral of centre in the metamorphosing animal (Fig. 18).

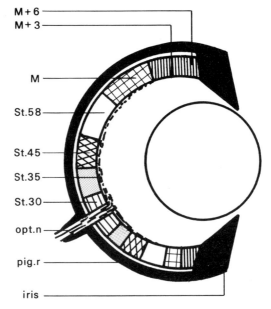

M + 6
M + 3
M
St.58
St.45
St.35
St.30
opt.n
pig.r
iris

Fig. 18
Diagram of the eye of a froglet six months after metamorphosis (M + 6) indicating the location of cells that were labelled at different stages of (larval) development[21]. For abbreviations see p. 76. (After Straznicky & Gaze[21]).

Contact between the optic cup at its iris margins and the overlying ectoderm loosens so that mesoderm can spread in under the ectoderm. These two superficial layers become the transparent cornea.

Mesodermal elements within the eye are the blood vessels that have entered through the choroid fissure and the intrinsic eye muscles.

Surrounding the eye are the mesodermal choroid coat (blood supply) and sclera (for support). The extrinsic eye muscles are believed by some to be the first three pairs of somites since their innervation is by the three most anterior ventral roots. This is by analogy with the trunk region where the motor or ventral roots of the spinal nerves innervate somites.

The neural crest

When the neural tube finally closes and the deep cells of the neural folds meet in the mid-line, a single column of cells is formed mid-dorsally (Fig. 11, ILD p. 27). The neural tube and overlying ectoderm are thus no longer in contact with each other. These cells, which were found at the lateral margins of the neural plate at the start of neurulation and dorsal to the newly formed neural tube at the end, are called neural crest cells.

The fate of these cells has been studied in many vertebrates and is so consistent that it is undoubtedly true in *Xenopus*.

In *Xenopus* it can be seen that the large neural crest of the head contributes to the visceral skeleton i.e. the skeleton of the jaws and gills. Posterior to the brain the neural crest can be seen to break up into clumps of cells with a segmental arrangement but still lying dorsal to the neural tube. Many of the cells start to migrate ventrally and stop in different positions on the way down. Other cells remain mid-dorsal and become the mesenchymal matrix of the dorsal fin.

In *Xenopus* the neural folds are quite shallow compared with those of Urodele neurulae in which many operations to remove the neural crest have been performed (p. 72). These extirpations result in a lack of certain cell types which leads one to the conclusion that the neural crest contributes to the formation of the following organs and cell types:

(a) Ganglia outside the C.N.S.
    i. Dorsal root ganglia
    ii. Sympathetic ganglia
    iii. Adrenal medulla
(b) Schwann cells
(c) Pigment cells (melanocytes)
(d) Visceral skeleton
(e) Dorsal fin

The cells which fall in categories (a)—(c) all have associations or characteristics in common with the nerve cells within the central nervous system, be they morphological (Schwann cells) or biochemical (adrenal medulla and melanocytes). Neural characteristics of group (d) and (e) cells are not so obvious.

References

21   Straznicky, K & Gaze, R M (1971). The growth of the retina in *Xenopus laevis*: an autoradiographic study. *J. Embryol. exp. Morp.* **26,** 67–79.

5 Development of Mesodermal Tissues after Gastrulation

IT will be remembered that the mesoderm lies within an equatorial crescent up to the start of gastrulation (the grey crescent). The cells of the mesoderm did not lie superficially as in other Amphibia but were located as a deep layer under endoderm and ectoderm in this region before starting to migrate inside the embryo[18]. Most mesodermal cells migrated to a dorsal position although the cells which invaginated over the ventral lip of the blastopore retained a ventral location.

During gastrulation the form of the mesoderm is as a sheet lying close to the dorsal endoderm and separated by a space, the blastocoel remnant, from the dorsal ectoderm. As such it is known as the mesodermal mantle. It is barely differentiated into the three major divisions, the notochord, somites and lateral plate, at the end of gastrulation. The prechordal plate, as its name implies, lies in front of the notochord. Its cells appear to be loosely arranged like a mesenchyme which lies between the pharynx, forebrain and anterior head ectoderm.

At stage 13 the mesodermal mantle may be separated into three regions behind the prechordal plate. The most dorsal median cells form a narrow 'rod' of coherent cells (the notochord). On each side, the mesoderm is arranged as an upper and lower sheet which are continuous with each other next to the notochord. This double mesoderm comprises somitic (most central) and lateral plate mesoderm. The mantle stretches from behind the forebrain to the blastopore.

Tissues to be derived from the developing mesoderm include the following:

1. the tadpoles axial skeleton from the notochord,
2. segmental structures like trunk musculature, vertebral arches and kidney tubules which either develop from the somites or are influenced by their proximity,
3. other mesodermal structures like the heart, blood vessels and blood, visceral muscles, part of the gonads and the limbs from lateral plate mesoderm.

Notochord

The notochordal cells form a discrete group as early as stage 13. At first the notochord is a narrow strip of tightly applied cells. It then becomes surrounded by the notochordal sheath and acts as the first axial skeleton of the embryo. The cells of the notochord do not divide frequently and early enlargement of the notochord is by a process of vacuolisation of its cells.

Vacuolisation during tail bud stages (20–30) accounts for elongation and straightening of the embryo. If the notochord is removed from a stage 13 embryo and the two sides of the embryo pressed together to heal the wound then a short and deformed embryo develops. It also seems to be abnormal in that the floor of the neural tube is thick and the somites meet in the mid-line. Such embryos cannot swim since there is no extended flexible structure which can be thrown into sinuous shapes by the muscles. If an operated embryo is stimulated physically its muscles will contract but the whole animal can do no more than contract and relax like a concertina.

As the embryo approaches metamorphosis elements from other meso-dermal tissues invade the notochord so that it becomes obsolete and disappears.

Somites

The cells which lie laterally to the notochord are also part of the meso-dermal mantle and can be divided into two groups. Those which lie closest to the notochord become elongated and form a horseshoe in transverse section. Attached to them at the open end of the horseshoe are lateral sheets of mesodermal cells arranged as a simple epithelium.

The spindle-shaped cells (Fig. 11a and b, p. 27) lying next to the noto-chord will segregate into blocks called somites. Somite formation in *Xenopus* is aberrant and unlike the process in other vertebrates[22]. In common with other vertebrates, segmentation starts anteriorly at the level of the front of the notochord and proceeds posteriorly at a regular rate. In *Xenopus* groups of cells, about ten cells long and elongated in the transverse plane, separate from the anterior end of the unsegmented paraxial mesoderm. The cells on each side then turn *en bloc* through 90 degrees. After this rotation, the long axes of the cells lie anteroposteriorly as can be seen in the transverse section in Fig. 11c and d. It is as though a section of the horseshoe shaped mass of cells partly opens out and the central ends of the cells move anteriorly while the lateral ends move posteriorly (Figs. 19 and 20). In this way the first pair of somites forms.

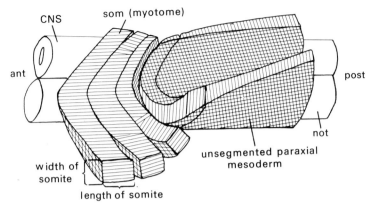

dorsal

CNS

som (myotome)

ant

post

not

width of somite

length of somite

unsegmented paraxial mesoderm

ventral

Fig. 19
Diagram of the mode of development of somites. (from Hamilton[22]).

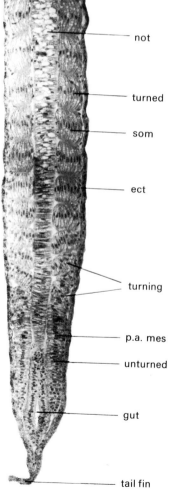

not

turned

som

ect

turning

p.a. mes

unturned

gut

tail fin

Fig. 20
Horizontal longitudinal section of *Xenopus* stage 28 embryo showing the formation of posterior somites from the paraxial mesoderm. For abbreviations see p. 76.

Somites form after this in an anterior posterior direction at about one pair per hour.

The last somites are segregated in the tail at stage 40, when there is a total of 45 post-otic somites. The four most anterior head somites which 'ie in front of the ear disappear one by one and all have disappeared by stage 47. The extrinsic eye muscles are thought to be of somitic origin in tetrapods. In *Xenopus* they may well be reincarnations of the first three pairs of somites which disappear by stage 30. Definitive eye muscles do not appear until their rudiments are visible at stage 39.

The initial function of the somites is one of locomotion for they form the axial musculature of the tadpole. Each myotome or muscle block *is* one somite and, provided the somites have some attachment to the notochord, either direct or indirect, and provided that the contractions of the somites are out of phase the tadpole will be able to swim.

In the well established feeding tadpole which has easily visible hind limb buds groups of cells which lie between the myotomes begin to surround the notochord and neural tube. These cells become chondrified and form the vertebrae. It will be appreciated that since the centres of the vertebrae lie between somites, each somite lies between two vertebrae and attaches to them (Fig. 21). When the somitic muscle contracts it will cause the vertebral column to bend. The cartilaginous vertebrae become bony at metamorphosis and their number is reduced to match the shorter axis and loss of the tail.

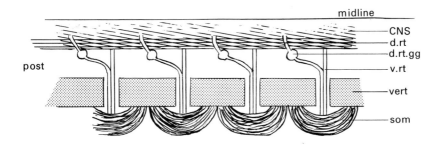

Fig. 21

Diagram of relationships between vertebrae, somites, CNS, dorsal and ventral root nerves. Dorsal view of right side of a vertebrate in the trunk regions.

The excretory system

The embryonic excretory organ develops at the level of head somites
3 and 4 and the first trunk somite. It is called either the pronephros or the
head kidney. It comprises segmentally arranged funnels which open into
the coelom and fine coiled tubules linking the funnel with a common
collecting duct. The funnels are ciliated but when the tubules become
further enlarged and coiled in the region of arterial buds (glomi) that
grow towards them, it is more likely that waste products diffuse from the
arteries than that they are wafted into the nephroi from the coelom.

The bilateral collecting ducts grow backwards by recruitment of local
cells[23] and finally reach anterior projections that grow out from the rectum.
All the ducts develop from solid strands of cells and all are open by
stage 37/38. The common collecting duct is also called the Wolffian duct.

The second and definitive kidney of *Xenopus* develops more posteriorly
than the pronephros. It is called the mesonephros.

Condensations of mesonephric cells appear on either side between the
endodermal mass and the myotomes. They soon differentiate into tubules
connected with the Wolffian duct. Well vascularised glomi appear. The
mesonephroi are first functional in the young feeding tadpole. Their
further growth is accomplished by the addition of two more sets of tubules
between those already present.

When the mesonephros is finally established as the tadpole's kidney, the
pronephros degenerates starting at stage 53. The leucocytes that infiltrate
the pronephros are also attracted to the anterior end of the mesonephros
which undergoes some degeneration, however, the tubules of this latter
region are soon regenerated.

The whole mesonephros is involved in changes during metamorphosis
and remodelling is not quite complete by the time the young froglet has
developed.

Lateral plate mesoderm—general

The lateral plate mesoderm is bi-layered, as mentioned previously.
At the end of gastrulation it occupies the most lateral parts of the mesodermal mantle and from there extends ventrally towards the mid-ventral
line. The two sheets of lateral plate mesoderm are only joined at their
ventral edge during their downward growth for when they meet mid-
ventrally these connections are severed and new ones are made between the
two inner portions and the two outer ones. Dorsally the two layers remain
connected. The outer layer or somatopleure becomes associated with the

body wall and the inner one or splanchnopleure associated with the gut. The cavity between them is called the coelom and the region where they are joined dorsally becomes the mesentery which supports the intestines. Fig. 22 indicates the diagrammatic relationship of all the mesodermal derivatives.

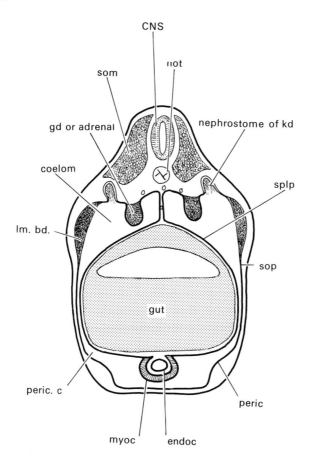

Fig. 22
Diagram showing the relationship of mesodermal structures in the developing larva. No one microscope section could pass through all the organs shown.

The heart and blood vascular system

The heart develops ventrally in the head from the most anterior lateral plate mesoderm. It originally develops under part of the pharynx, but as this latter enlarges the heart shifts backwards. In adult amphibia and other quadrupeds the heart lies under or behind the pectoral girdle.

The lateral plate mesoderm grows ventrally around the pharynx, one layer closely applied to the ectoderm and the inner layer close to the endoderm of the gut. Leading the downgrowth of the mesoderm round the pharynx are two groups of loosely arranged cells which meet mid-ventrally at stage 15. They remain an undifferentiated mass of cells until stage 27. The mid-ventral cells form the endocardial tube at stage 28 and are soon underlain by lateral plate mesoderm which has met mid-ventrally. At the same time the upper parts of this ventral mesoderm begin to fold up round the endocardial tube so as to enclose it. The anterior left and right coelomic cavities become confluent and together the space is called the pericardial cavity; the medial cells become the muscular myocardium and the outer epithelium the pericardium as is shown in Fig. 23.

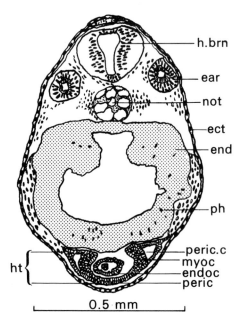

Fig. 23
Camera lucida drawing of a section through the developing heart region of a stage 29 embryo. For abbreviations see p. 76.

So far the heart is a blind tube with no connections, however, by stage 31 the endocardial tube has grown out forwards from the pericardium and branched. In this way the first two aortic arches which feed the gills are formed. The heart adopts an S-shape and a ventral ventricle can be distinguished from the atrium (Fig. 27). The atrium is divided by a septum at stage 45 (commencement of feeding) which separates the pulmonary return from the general venous return. The reason for such an arrangement in *Xenopus* is that the gills are used mainly for trapping food so that the lungs are established early as the organs of respiration.

The arteries develop as extensions of the major aortic arches but the veins develop somewhat later as channels for the return of blood that has reached peripheral organs like the pronephros.

The red blood corpuscles are nucleated throughout the life of *Xenopus* so that the state of maturity of *Xenopus* cannot be determined on morphology of the erythrocytes as it can be in mammals. However, the haemoglobin of the tadpole is different from that of the toad and at the time of metamorphosis both larval and adult haemoglobins can be recognised, sometimes in the same cell[24].

The gonads

The gonads develop as thickenings of the somatic mesoderm lying between the dorsal mesentery and the Wolffian duct. The mesoderm thus described forms all the elements of the gonad except the gametes and it is the hormones secreted by the former that determine the sex of the individual animals. *Xenopus* is typical of amphibia in that the female is the heterogametic sex. Young genetic males can be turned into fully fertile females by treatment with the appropriate hormones, and if these sex reversed males are bred with normal males all the offspring are males[25].

The primordial germ cells, which form the gametes, are derived from rather special endodermal cells that migrate up the dorsal mesentery and into the gonads between stages 43 and 46. Their further development either as oocytes or spermatocytes depends on the sexual differentiation of the animal.

At the beginning of embryonic development there is a region of the egg, located at the ventral pole, which is very rich in RNA. Cells developing in this region are also rich in the RNA which is simply divided between the cells that arise here during cleavage. When the fate of these cells is followed it is found that they become the primordial germ cells[26]. Consequences of this finding that have been verified experimentally are that

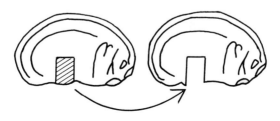

Fig. 24
Summary drawing of the operation for transfer of germ cells at stage 22[27].

appropriate regions of endoderm, and endoderm only, can carry genetic information with it when transplanted from one neurula to another[27] (Fig. 24). This cannot, of course, be finally tested until the host is mated and a second generation produced. Another test for the importance of the RNA rich cytoplasm in the development of germ cells is that afforded by ultraviolet light irradiation; for embryos developing from eggs irradiated at the vegetal pole are sterile when they grow up[28]

The hind limb

The lateral plate mesoderm provides the cells which will form all the components of the limbs except for the epidermis. However, the ectoderm,

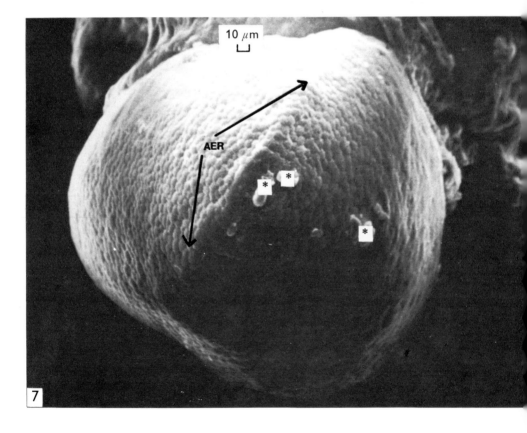

Fig. 25
Hind limb bud as seen with the scanning electron microscope at stage 51. For abbreviations see p. 76. Disregard the contaminating particles marked with asterisks. (From Tarin and Sturdee 26 in *Journal of Embryology and Experimental Morphology* by courtesy of the authors and the Company of Biologists.)

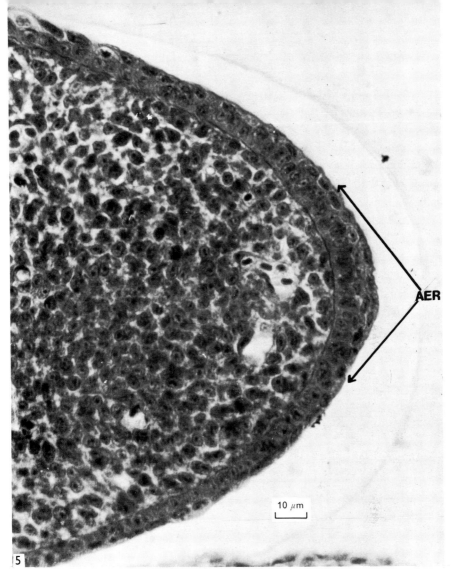

AER

10 μm

5

Fig. 26
Section through the apical ridge of the hind limb bud showing the thickening of the ectoderm at stage 51. (From Tarin and Sturdee[29] in *Journal of Embryology and Experimental Morphology* by courtesy of the authors and the Company of Biologists.)

if it behaves like that of other vertebrates, is of paramount importance in guiding the proper behaviour of the underlying mesodermal cells.

The first signs of hind limb development are manifested as collections of mesenchymal cells lying beneath the flank epidermis close to the anal canal[29]. The number of cells has increased so much by stage 48 that a small lump appears that can be seen with a low power dissecting microscope. A stage later the bud is larger and sections of it show that the ectoderm is quite thick and columnar in places.

The ectoderm of the limb bud becomes arranged so that a thickened ridge is formed at the tip. This so called apical ectodermal ridge can be seen very clearly in Figs. 25 and 26 and is the counterpart of the more pronounced ridge in the chick which is indispensible for chick limb development. This is the time (stage 51) when the first signs of the limb skeleton are visible, at the proximal end of the limb bud. The femur, then is the first skeletal element to be laid down. This is followed by the more proximal parts ending with the toes.

The limb muscles appear and form their attachments soon after the skeleton is formed.

References

22 Hamilton, L (1969). The formation of somites in *Xenopus. J. Embryol. exp. Morph.* **22,** 253–64.

23 Fox, H & Hamilton, L (1964). Origin of the pronephric duct in *Xenopus laevis. Arch. Biol. (Liège)* **75,** 245–51.

24 Jurd, R D & Maclean, N (1970). An immunofluorescent study of the haemoglobins in metamorphosing *Xenopus laevis. J. Embryol. exp. Morph.* **23,** 299–309.

25 Chang, C Y & Witschi, E (1956). Genic control and hormonal reversal of sex differentiation in *Xenopus. Proc. Soc. exp. Biol. Med.* **93,** 140–4.

26 Blackler, A W (1958). Contribution to the study of germ cells in Anura. *J. Embryol. exp. Morph.* **6,** 491–503.

27 Blackler, A W & Fischberg, M (1961). Transfer of primordial germ-cells in *Xenopus laevis. J. Embryol. exp. Morph.* **9,** 634–41.

28 Tanabe, K & Kotani, M (1974). Relationship between the amount of the 'germinal plasm' and the number of primordial germ cells in *Xenopus laevis. J. Embryol. exp. Morph.* **31,** 89–98.

29 Tarin, D & Sturdee, A P (1971). Early limb development of *Xenopus laevis. J. Embryol. exp. Morph.* **26,** 169–79.

6 Further Development of Endoderm Derivatives

ONCE the endoderm has invaginated it forms a blind tube open only at the posterior end. The blind end is surrounded by a thin layer of yolky cells and the cavity is wide. Further back the lumen is very restricted and lies at the dorsal side of the endodermal mass.

The yolk contained within the cells of the posterior part of the endoderm serves as nourishment for the embryo after the yolk and lipid supplies are depleted from the cells of the other parts of the embryo. The embryo cannot start to feed on external supplies of food until the mouth opens and it does this by confluence of a posteriorly growing invagination of ectoderm and a forward extension of the pharynx. The plate of cells

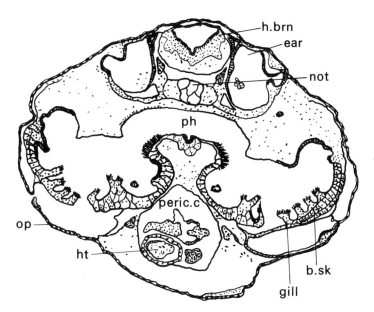

Fig. 27

Camera lucida drawing through a tadpole's pharynx–about stage 47–when the gills are the site for trapping suspended food. Water passes out of the pharynx through the gill slits and the hole in the operculum. For abbreviations see p. 76.

separating the buccal cavity from the pharynx ruptures at stage 40 but feeding does not begin until stage 45. The ability to feed coincides with the adoption of the typical head down swimming posture and it is important not to add food to the water until the tadpoles are old enough to take it.

The pharyngeal cavity enlarges greatly before feeding starts in order to accommodate the very large filter apparatus on the gills (Fig. 27). The intestines also become very long and coiled to cope with digestion of vegetable matter. The endoderm forms a simple epithelium throughout but it may be very folded in solid looking organs like the liver. However, the epithelial endoderm along the intestinal tract is always underlain by cells of the mesodermal splanchnopleure, even if it is not in the liver.

As will be seen in the next chapter many endodermal tissues will be destroyed or remodelled during metamorphosis.

7 Metamorphosis

ALMOST everyone has had the pleasure and excitement of watching a tadpole gain its front legs and lose its tail to become a frog. This change in form is so dramatic that the word metamorphosis, which means literally change of shape, is used to describe it.

The process of metamorphosis is a sudden affair occupying a period of a few days only, in *Xenopus*. The changes which take place are widespread and do not only affect the tail and limbs as a cursory glance might lead one to believe, for the animal also has to change internally to cope with life as a carnivore after having been a vegetarian.

The modifications involved in a change of diet, like the one mentioned, are very great. Normally a vegetarian's intestine is many times longer than that of a carnivore and *Xenopus* is no exception. There are about twenty coils in a tadpole's intestine which are reduced to one in the young frog.

Apart from its general length, the internal surface of the intestine in the tadpole, from about the stage when the tentacles arise, is increased by the development of the typhlosole. A similar structure is developed in the intestine of earthworms and in both cases may be described as a longitudinal fold within the intestine.

Reorganisation of the alimentary canal is very drastic and proceeds in an anterior posterior direction. The oesophagus is thus the first part of the gut to be altered. At stage 57 the glandular cells of the mucosa start peeling off and the epithelial cells begin to degenerate. Very soon most of the epithelium is degenerating to be followed by the regeneration of a simple epithelium. A new group of glandular cells appears and by stage 65 (last vestige of a tail) the lining of the oesophagus comprises a well developed epithelium containing many active glandular cells[30] (Fig. 28a and b).

The degeneration of the alimentary canal is noticeable in the duodenum (Fig. 28c and d) before it starts in the stomach at stage 59. It does not start in the ileum until stage 61, although here there are signs of a new population of epithelial cells *before* degeneration sets in. At the same time as

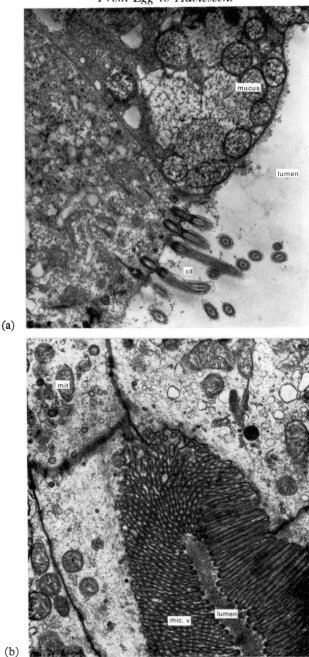

(a)

(b)

Fig. 28

Electron micrographs of the oesophagus and duodenum in the tadpole and after metamorphosis (a) Oesophagus at stage 48/49, × 14 000; (b) Oesophagus at stage 65, × 14 000; (c) Duodenum at stage 48/49, × 10 000; (d) Duodenum at stage 65, × 10 000. Notice in both cases, the loss of cilia and the gain of microvilli which may be associated with a change of diet. For abbreviations see p. 76. (By courtesy of Dr H Fox).

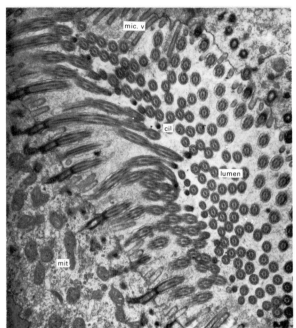

(c)

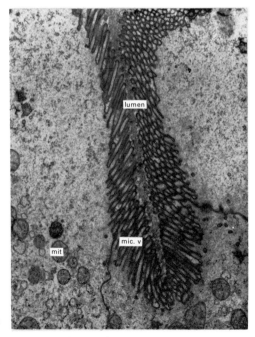

(d)

these cellular changes are taking place, the intestine is uncoiling. To accomplish this large number of cells must never be replaced after their dissolution. The last portions of the gut to be affected by the remodelling process are the colon, rectum and cloaca where degeneration begins at stage 63 and redifferentiation is complete at about stage 66.

Of the glandular derivatives of the endoderm some, such as the liver and gall bladder hardly change at all histologically, whereas the pancreas is almost completely destroyed. At stage 61, for instance, the pancreas looks like a sack full of degenerating cells, but there are a few scattered patches of healthy cells which later give rise to a complete 'new' pancreas. A similar drastic reorganisation of islet cells occurs at the same time.

The newly structured elements of the alimentary canal and its associated glands take on a modified function in an animal which only eats meat and a discussion of functional changes will be given later.

Changes in the skeleton and musculature of the head are necessary corollaries of the changes of diet described above. The tadpole's jaw structure has been an adaptation to filter feeding. The tadpoles have used their gills much less for respiration than collecting the small suspended particles on which they feed (Fig. 29). The cavity of the pharynx is enormous and in a large premetamorphic tadpole occupies about a quarter of the head and trunk. The mouth-slit is almost 10 mm in front of the eyes, and the eyes about 12 mm from each other.

By the end of metamorphosis the eye to mouth-slit distance is reduced and the distance between the eyes is now only about 7 mm. These changes are illustrated in Fig. 29. The figure also illustrates the changing position of the jaws and their articulation. The articulation of the jaws moves posteriorly so that the lower jaw itself shifts backwards. The palatoquadrate, with which the lower jaw articulates, changes its position from one in which it forms an anterior angle of 50 degrees with the cranium to one in which the angle is 115 degrees. The associated muscles are modified accordingly.

The most well-known morphological changes to take place are resorption and disappearance of the tail and the emergence of the forelimbs.

The tail is the organ of locomotion of the tadpole and its function is taken over by the strong swimming hind limbs which have been growing for most of the larval stage. The forelimbs have barely any locomotory significance but are of great use in feeding. A young *Xenopus* adult with deformed forelimbs may starve because it is unable to transfer food to its mouth. During their emergence, the forelimbs digest away the overlying skin so that they may reach the exterior. The tail is actually one of the last organs to show its metamorphic response. Perphaps this has evolved so that the breakdown products of gut renewal are a source of nutrition in the early stages of metamorphosis and the tail is later used as food while the shorter intestine is being finally remodelled for a meat diet.

The immediate stimulus for all these observed changes appears to be the hormones thyroxine and tri-iodothyronine secreted by the thyroid gland (Fig. 29). The thyroid gland in its turn is stimulated by the anterior pituitary.

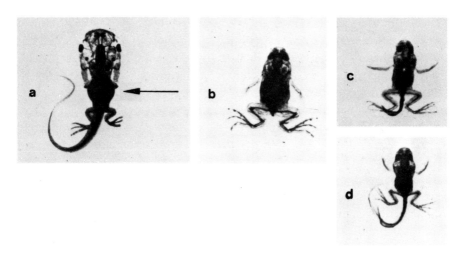

Fig. 29
These four *Xenopus* were treated in the following ways for 6 weeks starting at stage 52– (a) no thyroxine; (b) 12·5 μg/l thyroxine; (c) 6·25 μg/l thyroxine; and (d) 3·125 μg/l thyroxine The most concentrated solution had led to most rapid metamorphosis, (b), and the assumption of carnivorous feeding after metamorphosis was completed. The arrow in (a) indicates the position of the forelimb.

Many developmental biologists have been interested in elucidating the effects of these hormones on tissues that are known to respond to the metamorphic stimulus. The organs that have been studied in particular are the tail and the liver cell[31]. The tail of anuran tadpoles is extremely easy to keep alive when severed from the body and its reaction can, therefore, be studied in isolation. A *Xenopus* tadpole tail when isolated in this way will undergo the changes that are seen in the intact tadpole and it can be induced to 'metamorphose' at will[32]. An analysis of the reactions of the tail to thyroxine in the surrounding medium can readily be made (see Appendix, p. 73).

It has been discovered that thyroid hormones stimulate the synthesis of RNA and proteins in the tail before regression is observed. It is made more likely that these are the RNA and enzymes (protein) which are responsible for the regression itself by culturing tail tips and thyroid hormones together with metabolic inhibitors. The presence of actinomycin D (which inhibits RNA synthesis) or puromycin (which inhibits protein synthesis) with thyroxine in the culture medium prevents regression of the tail. The evidence points to a new synthesis of enzymes rather than the release of pre-packaged enzymes from lysosomes[31].

A similar study of liver cells and their assumption of a new battery of enzymes connected with a highly proteinaceous adult diet has been conducted. Once again, results indicate that thyroxine may be the natural agent stimulating this transformation.

One might have been able to deduce that there are big changes in the thyroid gland over the period which may be designated as metamorphosis. The cells lining the thyroid follicles are roughly cubical at the start of metamorphosis (with a side of about 7 μm—stage 58). The height of the follicle cells increases up to stages 62–64 when they measure 30μm, but are the same width[33]. The follicles themselves also increase in size and later decrease together with the height of the follicle cells. These are reduced to about 5 μm in the newly metamorphosed froglets. Throughout these changes in height the nucleus retains a central position with rough endoplasmic reticulum on the basal side and golgi vesicles on the follicular side. Mitochondria are found throughout the cell but are more common in the region of the endoplasmic reticulum. I think one might safely assume that the height of the thyroid cells indicate their degree of stimulation by pituitary hormones.

When thyroid cells are stimulated by pituitary hormones but cannot respond with sufficient amounts of thyroxine to damp down the secretion from the pituitary, the pituitary will continue to secrete thyroid stimulating hormone. A tadpole in which this has occured is shown in Fig. 30. It had been treated with an anti-thyroid drug which prevented the production of thyroid hormones. (The method for obtaining such tadpoles is described

15 mm

goitre

Fig. 30
Tadpole that has been reared in a 0·005 per cent solution of propylthiouracil for 9 months. Its untreated sibs would have metamorphosed about 6 months previously. (By courtesy of Dr R Coleman).

in the Appendix, p. 72). This led not only to an excess production of thyroid stimulating hormone, but an absence of metamorphosis in the now gigantic tadpole. The thyroid gland can be seen beneath the lower jaw of the tadpole and has enlarged enormously in a vain attempt to respond to the demands of the pituitary.

It is known that the various parts of the tadpole body have different sensitivities to thyroid hormones and it is of developmental advantage to the tadpole that this should be so. Sensitive tissues are those that show early changes like the oesophagus and more refractory ones like the tail require a more active thyroid before they are stimulated to change.

Many early investigators of metamorphosis in Anura discovered that treatment of tadpoles with thyroxine led to an unbalanced metamorphosis and death. They attributed this to the fact that the dose of thyroxine administered was well above the stimulatory level or 'threshold' for some of the reacting tissues. This meant that every responding organ or tissue would be undergoing dissolution at the same time and the animals would be truly 'messed about'.

However, in the normal situation, activity of the thyroid gland is graded so that vast changes in structure and function are brought about rapidly with the least inconvenience to the metamorphosing animal.

References

30 Fox, H, Bailey, E & Mahoney, R (1972). Aspects of the ultrastructure of the alimentary canal and respiratory ducts in *Xenopus laevis* larvae. *J. Morph.* **138,** 387–406.

31 Tata, J R (1971). Protein synthesis during amphibian metamorphosis. *Current topics in Developmental Biology.* **6,** Academic Press, 79–110.

32 Weber, R (1962). Induced metamorphosis in isolated tails of *Xenopus* larvae. *Experientia.* **18,** 84–5.

33 Coleman, R, Evennett, P J & Dodd, J M (1968). Ultrastructural observations on the thyroid gland of *Xenopus laevis* Daudin throughout metamorphosis. *Gen. comp. Endocrinol.* **10,** 34–46.

8 Regeneration

AMPHIBIANS have great powers of regeneration both in the adult and in the larva. Much work has been done using adult newts in which it has been found that new limbs may develop from the stump of old ones provided that the epidermis is intact. If the limb is amputated but otherwise undamaged, a normal limb will develop. On the other hand if the limb is cut through a heavily irradiated portion, it will heal but not regenerate. Regeneration therefore depends on the reproductive ability of cells lying at the cut surface.

Adult Anurans like *Xenopus* have a greatly reduced capacity for regeneration compared with Urodeles. However, the tadpole can regenerate the tail tip, the lens and the hind limb. Probably the easiest operation to perform is removal of the tail tip and the easiest regeneration to watch is that of the tail stump (Appendix 5. p. 76).

It can be seen that the wound is first closed by the spreading of the cut ends of the epidermis over the wound. Then the many dead or dying cells are cleared away. The notochord begins to lengthen as new cells are added from the cut end. Muscle cells develop but are not neatly segmented as were the myotomes. Then the tail fin grows out and becomes pigmented in the same way that the original tail was. Functionally the tail is as it was before; there are, however, persistent differences in muscle pattern and nerve layout.

A tail tip may be cultured *in vitro* after it has been cut off the tadpole. If such a tail tip is itself subjected to amputation, it has two points at which it can regenerate. In fact, when this is done, it can be seen that the tail attempts to regenerate at *both* cut surfaces[34]. The proximal end regenerates poorly in comparison with the distal end; but then one wouldn't expect a vertebrate's tail to regenerate the whole vertebrate!

Regeneration of the lens of the eye

The lens of a tadpole's eye may be carefully dissected out of the eyeball by making a small incision in the cornea and then hooking the lens out of the hole[35]. The wounded cornea heals in a day and a fully formed lens develops after a period of about two weeks. The stages of lens development are similar in the regenerating and the embryonic eye despite the fact that the cornea of the tadpole has an inner layer of mesenchyme of mesodermal origin.

The cornea of a tadpole eye is therefore made up of three layers; the outer two of which are continuous with the two layers of ectoderm which cover the whole external surface of the body. It is from the inner ectodermal layer that the new lens regenerates as depicted in Fig. 31.

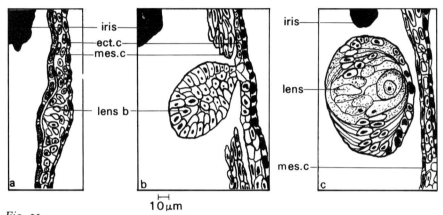

Fig. 31

Regeneration of the lens following its removal. In this case the new lens develops from the deep layer of the ectodermal cornea (a) and ruptures the mesodermal layer of the cornea (b) in its growth. When the lens severs its connection with the cornea (c), the mesodermal cornea can again bridge the gap. For abbreviations see p. 76. (After Freeman[35]).

The inner cornea forms a thickening of cells which bulges into the anterior chamber (Fig. 31a). The cells in this region divide rapidly so that a vesicle is formed which finally breaks through the underlying mesoderm. The lens rudiment is then free to expand further. The cells become arranged around a sphere which is still attached to the inner epithelium (Fig. 31b). The sphere of cells becomes larger and differentiated into long ones on the side away from the cornea and flatter ones next to the cornea. It is during this stage of the development of the regenerating lens that connection with the cornea is severed and mesenchymal cells come to cover the internal cornea again (Fig. 31c).

Further differentiation of the lens includes increase in volume and the synthesis of lens protein. Finally, this new lens occupies its normal position in the posterior chamber close to the iris.

In newts, a new lens develops from the dorsal iris, but although this site of lens regeneration is known in *Xenopus*, it is not the most common.

References

34 Hauser, R & Lehmann, F E (1962). Regeneration of isolated tails of *Xenopus* larvae. *Experientia.* **18,** 83–4.

35 Freeman, G (1963). Lens regeneration from the cornea in *Xenopus laevis. J. exp. Zool.* **154,** 39–65.

9 *Differentiation*

THE process of differentiation is often used to describe the final stages in the development of a cell type in which it assumes a characteristically mature state. Usually differentiated cells are unable to reproduce in adult animals but may be able to do so in immature or embryonic forms of the organism. For instance, one thinks of neural tissue and muscles being unable to divide when mature, and furthermore, that lost or dead cells cannot be replaced by addition of more cells but only by redeployment of those already present.

Differentiation should not be viewed so narrowly. Every step in development in which a cell has to make a choice in its future is one of differentiation. Every ectodermal cell during gastrulation will have to follow *either* the neural *or* the ectodermal pathway. Once a cell chooses to be neural it will develop into whatever cell type is characteristic of its location after a series of imposed choices.

If each *fully* differentiated cell has reached this state because ten of its antecedents had to make a simple yes/no choice, then there could be as many as 2^{10} or 1024 different cell types in the body.

Of course, a cell will sometimes die in the modelling of an organ and this can be considered as a choice facing the cell. There are many examples of programmed cell death and a few will be given here. The formation of spaces between the digits, the demise of the pronephros, the disappearance of the notochord and the massive death of intestinal and tail cells during metamorphosis all demonstrate the importance of cell death during development.

In every type of differentiation, except perhaps that consequent upon the separation of the egg's constituents during cleavage, the synthesis of a new mRNA is the first detectable chemical sign. In the early embryo the synthesis of mRNA coincides with the desynchronisation of cleavage which is rather abrupt.

When more specialised cell lines, which are characterised by the synthesis of specific proteins, develop there may be a lengthening of the cell

61

cycle. That is, there is a reduced incidence of cell division in cells which are about to differentiate. Is this because a cell which is differentiating uses its resources for RNA synthesis and specific proteins? Cells which appear to stop dividing early *viz.* somitic mesoderm, are among the first to differentiate. Muscle cells are thought to enlarge by becoming polynuclear or polyploid. Thus the nuclei or chromosomes divide but the cells do not. In this way the elaborate pattern of myofibrils is not disrupted and they continue to run the whole length of the cell. When a new source of muscle cells is required, to move the limbs for instance, it may be found among the undifferentiated members of the lateral plate mesoderm. Once a muscle is formed, it can only grow by enlargement as mentioned above. There do not seem to be any muscle cells that can act as a generative centre such as are found in adult intestinal epithelium, haemopoietic tissue etc. where the generative cell line is retained intact but half the daughter cells are side-tracked to form mature differentiated cells with a limited life span.

The cells of the tadpole retina are similar to those of the intestine in that division only takes place in cells at a particular location. A population of generative cells lies at the edge of the retina close to the iris. As these cells divide one remains where it is, may divide again, and then differentiates as a retinal cell; the other cell keeps to the retinal margin and remains an 'undifferentiated' stem cell. In consequence the oldest cells lie around the optic nerve and concentric rings of progressively younger cells surround them, terminating with the proliferative cells (Fig. 18).

In tadpoles we have seen that there may be a similar relationship between fully differentiated and undifferentiated, or dividing, cells as we find in the adult. However, the ratio tends to shift in favour of the differentiated cells in adult animals.

But what is the situation in early blastulae? It is known that the cells which lie under the grey crescent will develop the characteristics of mesoderm but it does not appear that mesoderm cells *know* what they are until they are invaginating into their definitive position.

If prospective mesoderm cells, lacking the dorsal lip of the blastopore, are transplanted to an ectodermal site they will not invaginate. Similarly, ectodermal cells will assume mesodermal properties if they are transplanted close to an invaginating dorsal lip.

These results lead us to the question of whether passage round the dorsal lip from exterior to interior of the embryo imbues an otherwise ectodermal cell with mesodermal properties. This cannot be the whole question because, as you may have discovered for yourself, prospective mesoderm of the early gastrula that has not yet invaginated, but is in contact with the dorsal lip, can induce neural tissues when it is placed within the blastocoel. It has reached the inside of the embryo without having traversed the dorsal lip. Now, could a piece of prospective mesoderm *without* attached dorsal lip do this? You can find out for yourself by appropriate modifications of the operation described in Appendix 2b, p. 70.

In the blastula, cells may have differentiated to the extent that they will form tissues of a particular type that may be determined by their position and/or their cell contents. They can be changed in their fate by proximity to other cells, and differences may later be observed in their cytoplasm. No one has yet been able to *see* differences in the nuclei of developing *Xenopus* embryos. However, it is now possible to investigate some of the developmental properties of the nuclei of embryonic amphibia.

Nuclear transplantation

The technique of nuclear transplantation has been pioneered and widely exploited in *Xenopus* by J B Gurdon[36].

The technique, in outline, is to kill the nucleus of newly laid but unfertilised eggs of *Xenopus* by ultraviolet light irradiation. These eggs act as hosts for embryonic cells derived from blastula onwards. Provided the donor cell is very slightly disrupted its nucleus can escape into, and take over the development of, the enucleated host egg (Fig. 32).

By experiments of this type Gurdon has shown that blastula and gastrula nuclei retain full potential for normal development. Nuclei from older cells like tadpole intestinal epithelium, can still promote normal development but at a reduced frequency. The reduced proportion of eggs transplanted with older nuclei that develop into normal toads can be explained by loss of nuclei or other failures of the operation. There may be no loss of developmental 'information' but it may be more difficult to expose it.

Nuclear transplantation studies have shown that any reproductive nucleus is capable of co-ordinating its division with that of the egg cytoplasm to yield an embryo which passes through the usual stages of development. This implies that the host egg cytoplasm either contains all the messages and controls for blastula formation, or it can elicit egg nuclear properties from the injected nucleus.

If the dogma expounded in chapters 1 and 2, that the amphibian egg contains the synthetic machinery necessary for early development is true, then foreign mRNA might be read off in the egg to produce a foreign protein. Gurdon *et al* injected haemoglobin mRNA into unfertilised eggs and did indeed find that haemoglobin is synthesised soon afterwards[37].

Similarly, the machinery is there to induce nuclei to incorporate

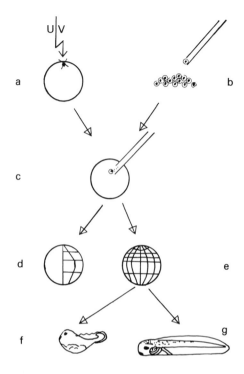

Fig. 32
Nuclear transplantation. The recipient oocyte's nucleus is inactivated with UV-light
(a). A donor cell is picked up from a dissociated blastula (b) and its cell membrane
broken by the tightly fitting pipette. This slightly broken cell is then injected into the
host oocyte (c). Cleavage may either be incomplete (d) or complete (e). In the latter
case the embryo may be imperfect (f) or normal (g).

tritiated thymidine (synthesise DNA) but it cannot induce adult brain
cells to do more than this. If adult brain cells do not resume a capacity to
multiply the host egg cytoplasm cannot divide. In this case it is impossible
to tell whether adult brain cells have lost their capacity to support development in other ways.

It therefore appears as though differentiation involves changes in
nuclear activity brought about by changes in the nuclear environment.
The cytoplasm is probably involved in transmitting information from the
external and internal environments to the nucleus, and then the cytoplasm
will react according to messages received from the nucleus, and may
produce compounds typical of a specialised differentiated cell. The
cytoplasm becomes developmentally limited but the nucleus remains
totipotent.

References

36 Gurdon, J B (1968). Transplanted nuclei and cell differentiation. *Sci. Amer.* **219,** (6), 24–35.

37 Gurdon, J B, Lane, C D, Woodland, H R, & Marbaix, G (1971). Use of frogs eggs and oocytes for the study of messenger RNA and its translation in living cells. *Nature.* **233,** 177–82.

10   *A Model for Development*

XENOPUS is perhaps not the best amphibian to choose for a book which is sub-titled 'A model for development'. Since Nieuwkoop and Florshutz[18] (see p. 30) publicised its aberrant gastrulation other authors have described different peculiarities.

The finding of the cells of both anterior and posterior origin in the posterior pronephric duct in *Xenopus* was not expected but the method of marking, using cells of different size and ploidy, had not been used on previous studies on the origin of the pronephric duct in other amphibia. Fox and Hamilton[23] (see p. 48) thought at first that the inclusion of local cells in the pronephric duct would apply to all amphibia but I do not feel this so strongly now for, once again, *Xenopus* may be aberrant.

The addition of somites was found to be so regular[22] (see p. 48) that the linear correlation of time with somites formed was the incredibly high figure of 0.995 (see Table 1).

Table 1

Data from Nieuwkoop and Faber 1956 showing the addition of somites with time. From Hamilton[22].

Age (h)	19.7	20.7	21.7	22.5	24.0	24.7	26.5	27.5	29.5
No. of somites	3.5	5	6.5	8.5	9.5	12	15	16	17

Age (h)	31.2	32.5	35.0	37.5	40.0	44.5	50.0	53.5	56.5
No. of somites	19	23	24.5	26.5	30	36	40	44	47

Hamilton[22] has shown conclusively that not only does *Xenopus* form its somites in a way that is abnormal for amphibia but for all vertebrates that have been inspected so far. This difference is shown very clearly in Fig. 33.

So much for these warnings not to take *Xenopus* as an example of amphibian development in every detail, but what is left of the development that may be taken as a 'model'? Of what does the reader *expect* it to be a model? Not of every type of animal development, because then the world would be populated with *Xenopus*. Not of isolated parts of development, for then we would not be studying the development of a whole.

What we *are* considering in reading this book is how one species has solved some of its problems of development. *Xenopus* may not gastrulate like a newt but it *does* gastrulate and having done so proceeds through the rest of its embryonic and tadpole stages until it metamorphoses into a young adult.

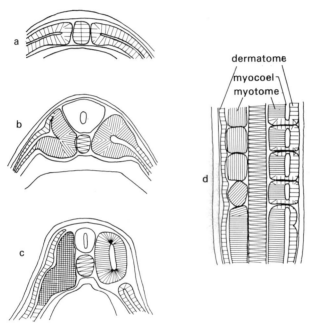

Fig. 33

A comparison of somite formation in *Xenopus* and other vertebrates. In all cases the pictures are a composite of *Xenopus* on the left and another vertebrate on the right. (a) Transverse section of late gastrula/early neurula. (b) Transverse section of early tail bud stage, posterior to sementation. (c) Transverse section through somites of tail bud stage. (d) Longitudinal section through segmented and unsegmented regions of an embryo. (From Hamilton[22]).

Appendix

ALL operations on amphibian embryos younger than hatching stage are permitted under the Antivivisection laws of Great Britain.

If you wish to manipulate tadpoles, you should consult your local Home Office Inspector and explain the procedure you wish to follow in the class.

1 Preparation of embryos for operations

(a) *Materials*

Embryos of the appropriate stage.

Watchmakers' fine forceps (e.g. Dumont 3 or 5).

Fine needles of glass or tungsten.

Hair loops (made by pushing two ends of a baby's hair into a finely drawn out pipette and sealing them in position with molten wax. If the wax forms a film across the loops, it can be broken loose before use).

Wide-mouthed pipettes (mouth *slightly* wider than naked embryo).

Splinters of cover slip glass.

70% alcohol for sterilising instruments.

30 mm Petri dishes lined with sterile 1% w/v Agar.

Sulphadiazine (May & Baker).

Lamp with heat filter e.g. with a special glass heat filter or a bottle of water interposed between embryos and the light source.

Sterile Holtfreter's solution.

(b) *Holtfreter's solution*

NaCl	3·5 g
KCl	0·05 g
$MgCl_2$	0·2 g
$CaCl_2$	0·1 g
$NaHCO_3$	0·2 g
distilled water	1 litre (glass distilled if possible).

(c) *Removal of egg membranes*

The *outer* jellies should be pulled off with forceps before the embryos, still clad in inner jelly membranes, are placed in Holtfreter's solution in an Agar lined dish. The inner jelly and vitelline membranes should be carefully removed using fine watchmaker's forceps. Remember to use a heat filter with the lamp.

Final removal of the jelly and vitelline membranes is tedious in *Xenopus* and should best be performed with deliberation. It is easier if a hold on the jelly is retained at all times particularly when just a small amount remains. Then, while still holding the last remnants of the jelly, the vitelline membrane may be pulled up slightly from the embryo's surface before it too is

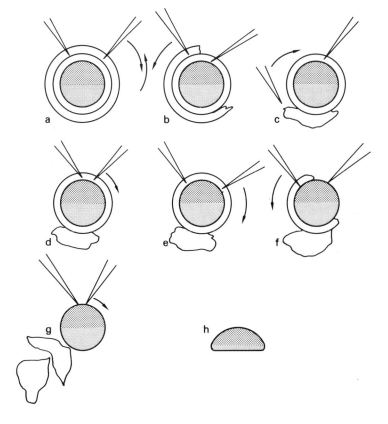

Fig. 34

Diagram of the removal of the jelly and vitelline membranes from a *Xenopus* embryo as viewed from the side. It is easier if a hold is retained on the egg membranes at all times. The diagram shows the outer sticky jelly being removed with a pull from each pair of forceps (a-c). The firmer inner jelly is then removed (d-f). Finally the vitelline membrane is split by pulling the forceps gently apart (g) thus liberating the embryo (h). Denuding a young embryo is not as easy or quick as this.

grasped (through the remaining jelly) with both pairs of forceps. The forceps are then gently, but surely pulled away from each other until the membrane splits and the embryo pops out. Skill in removing the jelly and vitelline membranes requires practice and a steady hand.

The embryos should then be transferred in a wide-mouthed pipette to a clean Agar lined dish and medium. The mouth of the pipette on transfer must be placed *in* the liquid for if a naked embryo touches the surface of the liquid it will be dispersed over it.

Any slight wounds on the embryo occasioned by decapsulation will heal within a few minutes.

The following films may be of help and interest:

Two classical operations on amphibian embryos. (1) *Neural crest removal from an axolotl embryo,* and (2) *Implantation of the dorsal lip of the blastopore into the blastocoel in Xenopus.* This is a very clear film of the operations in question and demonstrates well the method of operating on young embryos. A Darbishire/Hamilton Production.

It is a 16 mm silent, colour film which runs for about 10 minutes. It may be bought from Gratton Darbishire, The Lawns, Byfield, Nr Daventry, Northamptonshire, UK or it may be hired from the Higher Education Film Library, Scottish Central Film Library, 16–17 Woodside Terrace, Glasgow G3 7XN.

The other film is entitled *Gastrulation and neurulation in the amphibian embryo: Xenopus laevis.* It too is a 16 mm film and runs for 11·5 minutes. It may be hired or purchased from Dr D Tarin, Department of Anatomy, The School of Medicine, Leeds LS2 9NL.

2 Operations on early embryos

(a) *Exogastrulae* (p. 29. 2).

Embryos at stage 8 (late blastula) are demembranated as described above. After rinsing in Holtfreter solution they should be put in Agar lined dishes containing *double* strength Holtfreter solution and sulphadiazine at a concentration of about 1:1000. Watch the embryo's development up to the time that untreated embryos have reached about stage 22.

(b) *Implantation of the dorsal lip of the blastopore* (p. 29. 3).

Two early gastrulae (stage 10) are selected for the operation and demembranated (Appendix 1c). The least damaged one should be the host. They should both be placed in the same Agar lined dish under full strength Holtfreter's solution.

The donor should be turned upside down so that the dorsal lip can be seen. The host remains animal pole uppermost so the blastocoel is easily accessible. Text-book embryos are always represented as spheres; however, when the jelly and vitelline membranes have been removed, gastrulae look rather flattened like tam o'shanters.

While the dorsal lip is cut away with a fine needle, the embryo is held firmly but gently with a hair loop. When the dorsal lip material has been freed from the donor, it is cut into a few smaller pieces, for the host blastocoel cannot accommodate a whole dorsal lip.

One of the small pieces is then moved to the host embryo.

A slit is cut in the host's blastocoel roof and the piece of dorsal lip inserted.

Sometimes the wound gapes and it is necessary to press the cut edges together by applying splints. These are small pieces of glass broken from a cover slip and pushed into the agar to form tight walls around the embryo.

After about an hour the wound should have healed and the glass can be removed.

The healed embryo can then be pipetted gently into another Agar lined dish containing 50% Holtfreter's solution, and thence by gradual dilution to 10% Holtfreter's. Bacterial and fungal infection can be reduced post-operatively by the addition of sodium sulphadiazine to the culture medium at a dilution of 1:1000.

The developing embryo can be observed over the next few days for signs of secondary induction, particularly in the belly region.

(c) *Vital staining*

As mentioned in the text (p. 29. 1) *Xenopus* embryos are not the best material for vital staining since the future mesoderm lies beneath the surface in a stage 8 blastula. However, the method is as follows:

Coloured Agar strips are made at least a *week before* the practical exercise.

Dissolve 2 g of Agar powder in 100 ml of distilled water. Divide into two approximately equal portions. To one portion add 0·5 g neutral red and to the other 0·5 g nile-blue sulphate. Rest glass plates at a shallow angle on absorbent paper and then pour a layer of red or blue Agar over each one. Allow the Agar to dry.

Chip the dry coloured Agar off the plates or add a drop of water to the edge and peel it off. Store the dried coloured Agar in air-tight containers.

Make a soft paraffin base for a small Petri dish and work some embryo-sized depressions in it. Place alternate snippets of coloured Agar in it. Then a de-jellied embryo (still in its vitelline membrane) is laid in the depression. 10% Holtfreter's solution is then gently added to the required depth. After an hour the embryo is carefully removed from the hole and put in a clean dish with medium. A drawing of the positions of dye spots are now made so that they may be followed through gastrulation.

3 **Neural crest removal** (p. 36)

The operation should be performed on embryos of stages 14–16 when the neural folds, in which lie the neural crest cells, are high and well separated. The regions of neural folds to be removed are those parts of the ridges which lie in the posterior half of the embryo.

The embryos should be transferred from the demembranating dish (Appendix 1c) to a clean Agar-lined Petri dish containing full strength Holtfreter's solution. A shallow trough may be made in the Agar to help steady the embryo during the operation.

The cells of the neural fold are rather sticky and have to be coaxed free. After the folds, with their contained neural crest cells, have been removed, the wounds heal quite quickly and neurulation proceeds.

The excised neural crest may be cultured successfully *in vitro* and will produce those cells that should be absent from the embryo and larva e.g. pigment cells and dorsal tail fin among others.

4 **Metamorphosis**

Tadpoles may be hastened or delayed in their passage through metamorphosis by treatment with thyroxine or an antagonist to thyroxine. In every case where tap water is used, it should be allowed to stand for 24 hours before solutions are made up and it is put to use.

(a) *Speeded up metamorphosis* may be obtained by rearing stage 59 tadpoles in a medium (tap water) to which 0·0125 mg/litre of *thyroxine* has been added. Different dilutions of thyroxine should be used and the effects of each compared with normal metamorphosis (Fig. 29). Feeding should proceed as usual.

(b) *Inhibition of metamorphosis* can be obtained by rearing stage 50 tadpoles in a 0·005% solution of *propylthiouracil* in standing tap water. After about nine months of regular feeding a monster tadpole such as that shown in Fig. 30 may be produced.

The culture medium for 4 *a* and *b* should be changed at least once a week.

5 **Regeneration of the tail** (p. 60)

Hauser and Lehmann[33] have described a method of removing the tailtip of tadpoles so that it can be cultured separately while the tadpole is regenerating its own tail.

The tadpole should be left, in aqueous 0·05% sulfothiazol (Geigy) (0·001% sulphadiazine will do) for one day. The tadpole should then be thoroughly *rinsed* in *distilled water* before the tip of its tail is cut off and put into a small quantity of Holtfreter solution containing 0·05% sulfoth-iazol. The tadpole can be returned to its usual culture.

The tail of the tadpole will regenerate in one or two weeks and the isolated tail may show signs of tail regeneration. The tail is able to swim and may live about a month at 18°C.

If necessary, tadpoles may be anaesthetised in 1:5000 MS 222. Such isolated tails of tadpoles can be induced to undergo metamorphic changes by exposing them to dilutions of thyroxine of about $1:10^6$ or $1:5 \times 10^6$ concentration (p. 55).

Glossary

Adrenal medulla — that part of the adrenal gland which secretes adrenalin in response to nervous stimulation.

Axolotl — a salamander. One which becomes sexually mature without losing its larval body structure.

Axon — the long conducting process of a nerve cell. Often refers only to the process which conducts nerve impulses away from the nerve cell body.

Blastomere — one of the first cells in the embryo.

Blastocoel — the first cavity in an embryo that is formed centrally when the blastomeres are being separated from each other.

Chiasma (ta) — The point(s) at which crossing over takes place in meiotic chromosomes.

Chondrified — made into cartilage.

Cortex (egg) — the cytoplasm that lies immediately under the cell membrane.

Ectopic — lying away from its normal position.

Epiboly — spreading of the future epidermis over the rest of the embryo during gastrulation.

Erythrocyte — red blood cell.

Genome — the totality of all the genes in an individual.

Golgi vesicle — part of the membranous structure of a cell. Can be best demonstrated with the electron microscope.

Grey crescent — site of origin of mesoderm. It can be seen after fertilisation just above the equator (see p. 14 for its formation).

Haemopoietic tissue — groups of cells involved in the formation of blood cells.

Leucocyte — white blood cell.

Lysosome — intracellular organelle which contains enzymes capable of digesting that cell.

Melanocyte — black pigment cell.

Mesenchyme — loosely packed cells that lie between other more distinct cell masses.

Metamorphosing — undergoing metamorphosis (see Chapter 7).

Myofibril — minute element that runs along and within a muscle cell. Mechanically responsible for muscle contraction.

Neural crest — cells that lie in the raised fold that demarcates the junction between epidermis and future central nervous system (see p. 36).

Oocyte — immature egg cell in ovary and also after laying while still unfertilised.

Oogenesis — development of the oocyte within the maternal organism. (Chapter 1).

Phase contrast microscope — a microscope adapted for looking at small living unstained objects.

Pineal body — a single dorsal outgrowth of the brain. Becomes the third eye in some reptiles.

Primordial germ cell — a cell which is destined, from a very early age, to become eggs or sperm.

Pronuclei — nuclei of egg and sperm before they fuse to become the zygote nucleus.

Schwann cells — by means of their cell membranes make up the 'fatty' insulation around nerve axons.

Sub-cortical — lying just beneath the egg cortex.

Typhlosole — an internal flap of intestinal epithelium that enlarges the functional surface area.

Vacuolisation — increasing the number of vacuoles. May increase the total volume of a cell by adding 'dead' space.

Vitelline membrane — extracellular material lying between the oocyte and follicle cells; and later between the egg and jelly.

Yolk platelet — minute particle within the large oocyte and embryonic cytoplasm that supplies nutrition necessary for early development.

Zygote — the embryo after conjunction of egg and sperm nuclei but before cell division.

Abbreviations used in Figures

A.E.R.	apical ectodermal ridge	mic.v	microvillus
ant	anterior	mit	mitochondrion
arch	archenteron	myoc	myocardium
bcl	blastocoel	n.cr	neural crest
bip.c	bipolar cell	not	notochord
brn	brain	n.t	neural tube
b.sk	branchial skeleton	nuc	nucleus
c.gr	cortical granule	nucol	nucleolus
cil	cilium	nuc.p	nuclear pore
CNS	central nervous system	op	operculum
d.l.b	dorsal lip of the	opt.c	optic cup
	blastopore	opt.n	optic nerve
d.rt	dorsal root	opt.v	optic vesicle
d.rt.gg	dorsal root ganglion	p.a.mes	paraxial mesoderm
ect	ectoderm	peric	pericardium
ect.c	ectodermal cornea	peric.c	pericardial cavity
end	endoderm	ph	pharynx
endoc	endocardium	pig.r	pigmented retina
fol	follicle cell	p.gr	pigment granule
f.t	furrow tip	post	posterior
gd	gonad	rec.c	receptor cell
gg.c	ganglion cells	ret	retina
gl	gill	rib	ribosome
gl.p	gill pouch	sens.r	sensory retina
h.brn	hind brain	som	somite
ht	heart	sop	somatopleure
kd	kidney	splp	splanchnopleure
l.b.c	lamp brush chromosome	t.j	tight junction
lens b	lens blastema	v.l.b	ventral lip of the
lm.bd	limb bud		blastopore
l.pl	lateral plate	vert	vertebra
mac.v	macrovillus	v.rt	ventral root
mes	mesoderm	yk.pt	yolk platelet
mes.c	mesodermal cornea		

Index